AN
INWARD
JOURNEY

PETER KNOESTER

Cover Design by: Authors Hike

Publisher: Authors Hike

For permission requests, please contact: peter.knoester@hotmail.com

Table of Contents

Chapter 1
An Inward Journey

Are we part of a herd, guided by unseen forces, moving in a direction we rarely question? Do we simply follow the paths set before us without truly understanding why? The world's religions—Islam, Buddhism, Hinduism, Christianity, and others—each offer their own way of connecting with the Creator. While their teachings differ, they share a fundamental truth: humanity has an inherent longing for something beyond the material world, a desire to understand our purpose and seek unity with the Divine.

Within Christianity, this search for God has led to numerous divisions. The Christian church, once united under the teachings of Jesus and His apostles, has splintered over centuries, creating various denominations, each with its own interpretations. While the core message of Christ remains, theological differences have emerged, sometimes obscuring His original teachings.

I realize this is a bold claim, but from my perspective, the path to knowing the Creator is through Christ, as presented in biblical history. My upbringing was in the Christian faith, yet I acknowledge my imperfections. There were times when I strayed so far that returning seemed impossible, yet here I am, reflecting on my spiritual journey. Perhaps there are others who feel the same—those who question, struggle, and seek deeper understanding.

This inner longing for meaning, this urge to seek something greater than ourselves, is not unique to any one person or religion. It is a universal force woven into the fabric of existence. Many belief systems recognize this longing in their own ways. In Hinduism, the ultimate goal is moksha, liberation from the cycle of rebirth and unity with the divine source, Brahman. Buddhists strive for enlightenment, reaching a state of spiritual awakening that frees them from suffering and ignorance. Muslims seek closeness to Allah through faith, prayer, and righteous living, believing that true fulfillment comes from submission to God's will. In Judaism, a deep connection with God is achieved through devotion to His laws and moral living. Similarly, in Christianity, this yearning is often understood as the soul's desire to reunite with its Creator, made possible through the teachings and sacrifice of Jesus Christ.

Even nature reflects this principle. Birds migrate vast distances without needing instruction, fish swim against strong currents, and plants instinctively reach toward the light—all driven by an unstoppable force that compels them to grow and fulfill their purpose. Some call it instinct; others attribute it to natural law. I believe it is a reflection of the Creator's design, a reminder that all living things possess an urge to expand, thrive, and ultimately find their place within the greater order of existence.

While different religions offer varying perspectives on how to connect with the Divine, they share a common theme: the search for something beyond this world. Understanding these similarities can foster respect and dialogue between faiths rather than division. We may walk different paths, but the longing for spiritual truth unites us all.

The expression "the grass is always greener on the other side" often defines the human condition. Many of us are never truly satisfied with what we have, always yearning for something beyond our current state. This restless longing, this constant urge for more, is deeply ingrained in all living things. Just as plants stretch toward the sun and rivers carve new paths through the earth, so too do humans seek growth—spiritually, intellectually, and emotionally. But where does this urge lead us? For many, it is the pursuit of material success or personal fulfillment; for others, it is the journey toward something greater—the search for the Divine.

This search, however, is not a straightforward one. Across the world, people follow different religious paths, each shaped by their upbringing, culture, and historical traditions. The way we seek God is often influenced by where we are born. A child raised in a Hindu family may grow up learning about dharma (righteous duty) and karma (cause and effect), while a child in a Muslim household is taught about Tawhid (the oneness of God) and the Five Pillars of Islam. Christians are brought up believing in Christ as the Redeemer, while Buddhists seek Nirvana, a state of liberation from suffering. As children, we follow the beliefs of our parents, rarely questioning them. It is only when we grow older—when we begin to think critically about the world and our place in it—that we start asking deeper questions: Is this the right path? Is there only one way to know God?

With so many religious traditions, it is easy to feel lost. Every faith offers a means of reaching the Divine, yet the paths vary greatly. Some believe that devotion and righteous living bring us closer to God, while others emphasize prayer, meditation, or acts of service. Christianity teaches that the way to the Creator is through Jesus Christ, whose sacrifice cleanses believers of sin and grants them eternal life. In contrast, Judaism, which follows the Old Testament, sees the covenant between God and the Jewish people as central to spiritual fulfillment. The Torah—the foundation of the Jewish faith—outlines laws, ethics, and traditions meant to keep the people in alignment with God's will.

Historically, in Judaism, sins were atoned for through sacrificial offerings. A lamb, a dove, or another pure animal was presented at the temple, its blood symbolically cleansing the people of wrongdoing. This practice, carried out by the high priest, was seen as a means of restoring harmony with God. In Christianity, this tradition finds its ultimate fulfillment in Jesus Christ, whom believers see as the final and ultimate sacrifice. His death on the cross, according to Christian teaching, replaced the need for continual offerings, allowing all who accept Him to be forgiven and granted eternal life in heaven.

Religions differ in their methods, but the underlying truth remains: humanity seeks connection with its Creator. The longing to understand our purpose, to bridge the gap between the seen and the unseen, is universal. Whether through the path of Christ, the adherence to religious laws, the pursuit of enlightenment, or the call to prayer, all faiths acknowledge that there is something beyond this temporary world—a greater reality that calls to the human soul. The challenge lies in choosing the path that resonates most deeply, in finding the way that leads us to true fulfillment.

Chapter 2
Religion Made Easy

To say that religion is a simple matter would be misleading. Faith is not merely a set of beliefs but a way of life, requiring dedication, discipline, and adherence to certain principles. Every major religion—Christianity, Islam, Hinduism, Buddhism, and Judaism—offers a framework for understanding human existence and, in most cases, a path to eternal life or spiritual liberation beyond this world.

As a Christian, I firmly believe in an afterlife, a place where the soul continues its journey beyond the physical realm. Many have sought to understand and describe what awaits us after death. Countless books have been written, filled with personal testimonies of divine encounters, near-death experiences, and visions of heaven. Yet, in Christianity, the primary source of knowledge about salvation and eternal life is the Bible—a sacred text deeply connected to the Torah, the foundation of Jewish scripture.

The Christian Bible is divided into two parts: the Old Testament, which largely aligns with the Jewish Torah, and the New Testament, which focuses on the life and teachings of Jesus Christ. The Old Testament recounts the origins of humanity, the history of the Israelites, and the guidance given to them through the prophets, who foretold the coming of a Messiah—a savior who would redeem the world. For Christians, Jesus is the Messiah, the one whose life, death, and resurrection offer the ultimate path to eternal life.

While Christianity teaches that salvation comes through Christ's sacrifice, other religions offer different perspectives on the afterlife. Islam, for instance, teaches that after death, a person's deeds will be weighed, and they will either enter Jannah (paradise) or face judgment. Hindus believe in reincarnation, where the soul is reborn based on its karma, striving ultimately for moksha, liberation from the cycle of birth and rebirth. Buddhists seek nirvana, a state of ultimate peace and enlightenment, free from suffering and worldly attachment. Judaism, unlike Christianity, does not focus as much on the afterlife but emphasizes living a righteous life according to God's laws, with varying beliefs about what happens after death.

For Christians, the concept of the Trinity—God the Father, God the Son (Jesus Christ), and God the Holy Spirit—is central to salvation. This is a profound and complex doctrine, emphasizing that God is one being in three persons, each playing a role in humanity's spiritual journey. God the Father is the Creator, Jesus Christ is the Redeemer who sacrificed Himself for humanity's sins, and the Holy Spirit is the guiding presence that transforms believers from within. This transformation, often called being "born again," is not merely a religious ritual but a deep, spiritual renewal where a person surrenders their old self to live according to God's will.

Ultimately, the relationship between creation—you and I—and the Creator is of the highest importance. Whether through Christianity, Islam, Hinduism, or other faiths, people seek connection with the Divine, striving to understand their place in the grand design of existence. The paths may differ, but the desire for truth, purpose, and eternal peace unites us all.

As human beings, our perception is often limited—we rarely see beyond the immediate reality in front of us. Our understanding of existence, purpose, and the divine is like looking through a dark glass, as the Apostle Paul describes, where we only catch glimpses of the full truth. However, in Christian belief, when the Holy Spirit enters a person's heart, it illuminates the soul, revealing the path to eternal life.

This transformation is not always immediate or fully comprehensible, but it begins a journey toward spiritual awakening, guiding the believer toward a deeper understanding of God's will.

In Christianity, this divine revelation is made possible through the Trinity—God the Father, God the Son (Jesus Christ), and God the Holy Spirit—who work together to bring salvation and enlightenment. The Holy Spirit acts as a bridge between the divine and the human soul, offering wisdom, comfort, and the ability to discern spiritual truths that might otherwise remain hidden.

Many spiritual traditions also speak of divine enlightenment or awakening. In Buddhism, nirvana is the ultimate realization, where one transcends suffering and ignorance. Hinduism teaches about Atman (the true self) and its connection to Brahman (the ultimate reality), which is gradually revealed through meditation, devotion, and self-discipline. In Islam, divine guidance comes through Allah's revelations in the Quran, with the light of faith leading believers toward righteousness. Even Judaism, which emphasizes the covenant between God and His people, speaks of spiritual insight being granted through study, prayer, and adherence to divine commandments.

Across all these traditions, people seek enlightenment—whether it is through the Holy Spirit, inner meditation, divine scripture, or moral discipline. Throughout history, countless books have been written by those who have experienced profound spiritual transformations. Their testimonies and insights provide valuable perspectives, helping seekers navigate their own journey toward divine truth. Whether through personal experiences, sacred texts, or philosophical reflections, engaging with these writings can deepen our understanding of eternity, faith, and the unseen realities beyond our limited vision.

Chapter 3
Thoughts About Heaven

A s I sit here at my computer, I find myself trying to envision what heaven is like—what it truly means, what it holds, and what existence in such a place would be. I have attempted to describe it in some of my previous writings, but the reality is that no one can fully comprehend heaven. It is beyond human experience, beyond our limited understanding, beyond what words can truly capture.

One thing I am certain of, however, is that heaven is a place of purity— a realm where, for lack of a better word, nothing *unclean* can enter. This is a central belief in Christianity, where heaven is described as the dwelling place of God and the redeemed, those who have been cleansed through faith in Christ. The Bible, particularly in the Book of Revelation, speaks of a place without pain, sorrow, or sin, where those who are saved live in eternal joy, praising God.

Yet, as human beings, we think in earthly terms. Our entire perception of life is shaped by the physical world—what we see, touch, and experience daily. But heaven is a spiritual realm, something entirely different from the material existence we know. I do not believe that we will have earthly bodies there, at least not in the way we understand them now. The Bible speaks of a transformed, glorified body, something far beyond our present physical form.

When discussing heaven with a friend, I casually remarked that there are no computers in heaven—a statement that, at the time, felt trivial, even humorous. But upon deeper reflection, it led me to consider the nature of existence beyond this life. What will we do in heaven? How will time function? Are there days, or is it an eternal present? These are questions that have intrigued theologians and philosophers for centuries, and they remain largely unanswered.

While Christianity speaks of heaven as a place of eternal communion with God, other religious traditions offer different perspectives on what happens after death.

- In Islam, Jannah is described as a paradise where the faithful are rewarded with peace, joy, and closeness to Allah. The Qur'an describes it as a garden of eternal bliss, where the righteous dwell in the presence of God, free from earthly suffering.

- Hinduism teaches that the ultimate goal is moksha, or liberation from the cycle of birth and rebirth. Rather than a physical paradise, this is a state of unity with Brahman, the ultimate reality, where the soul is freed from all worldly attachments.

- Buddhism does not traditionally focus on a "heaven" in the way Christianity or Islam does. Instead, nirvana represents the end of suffering and desire, a state of complete spiritual enlightenment where one transcends the cycle of existence.

- In Judaism, the concept of the afterlife is more nuanced. Some Jewish traditions speak of Olam Ha-Ba ("the World to Come"), a place of reward for the righteous, while others focus more on the idea of resurrection and a future messianic age rather than a distinct heaven.

Despite these differences, a common theme runs through all these beliefs: the idea that life is not just about the here and now, but that something greater awaits beyond death. Whether it is eternal communion with God, spiritual liberation, or enlightenment, most religious traditions affirm that there is more to existence than what we currently perceive.

What is it that binds us all together in the next life? Will it be the fact that we were saved through the Son of God and share in the redemption He provided? Or will we reach a state where we no longer need to speak to each other because we will fully understand everything, just as God does?

The idea of knowing everything is both exciting and overwhelming. If heaven is truly a place without confusion, doubt, or unanswered questions, will we even need to ask anything? Or will we simply understand all things without the need for words? It is hard to imagine, but perhaps that is the point. As humans, we have limits to what we can understand, and heaven is beyond those limits.

Jesus spoke about heaven as a house with many mansions, a place prepared for those who follow Him. But could this mean something deeper than just a place to live? Maybe it represents the vastness of eternity, where every soul finds its perfect place with God. Many people think of heaven as a joyful reunion with loved ones, a paradise, or an endless celebration. The truth is likely greater than anything we can imagine.

It is easy to think of the afterlife as a happy ending, like the final page of a book where everything turns out well. But maybe eternity is not an ending at all. Maybe it is the beginning of something far greater than we can imagine.

No matter how much I think about it, I cannot fully explain what is unknown. But maybe faith does not require full understanding. Maybe all we need to know is that what comes next will be greater than anything we can ever dream of.

Chapter 4
The King or Ruler of this World

A Deeper Exploration

In the New Testament, Christ makes a profound statement about "the ruler of this world," indicating that this entity has no claim over Him. Many Christian theologians and believers interpret this to mean Satan, the adversary of God and mankind. From the very beginning, as described in Genesis, Satan was present in the Garden of Eden, deceiving the first human beings into disobeying their Creator. This singular act of rebellion had catastrophic consequences, bringing sin, suffering, and death into the world. Humanity, originally intended to live in eternal communion with God, was instead subjected to the weight of sin and the inevitability of physical and spiritual death.

The Role of Satan in Human History

Satan, described in various parts of the Bible as "the father of lies" (John 8:44), has continuously worked to keep humanity from the truth. Through deception, he influences nations, cultures, and individuals. His intelligence and cunning nature allow him to manipulate through various means—be it through ideology, entertainment, materialism, or even within religious institutions that deviate from divine truth.

In Christian belief, Satan's primary objective is to keep people away from the path of salvation. He does this by enticing individuals with distractions, worldly pleasures, and falsehoods that appear appealing but ultimately lead away from God. This is why many Christians believe that the struggle between good and evil is not merely physical but deeply spiritual—a battle for the souls of humankind.

The Path to Redemption Through Christ

Christian doctrine holds that salvation from the power of Satan came only through Jesus Christ. The arrival of Christ, His death on the cross, and His resurrection are seen as the ultimate victory over sin and death. Christ's sacrifice provided a way for humanity to escape eternal separation from God. As John 3:16 states, "For God so loved the world that He gave His only begotten Son, that whosoever believes in Him shall not perish but have eternal life."

For those who follow Christ, the path to eternal life is through faith in Him, repentance from sin, and adherence to His teachings. The New Testament frequently emphasizes that spiritual warfare is ongoing. Ephesians 6:12 states, "For we wrestle not against flesh and blood, but against principalities, against powers, against the rulers of the darkness of this world, against spiritual wickedness in high places." This highlights that the struggle is beyond the physical realm—it is a battle for spiritual truth.

The Influence of Satan in the Modern World

It is often said that Satan influences the structures of the world—be it through media, politics, entertainment, or personal temptations. In many Christian teachings, the concept of spiritual deception is crucial. There is an understanding that Satan uses various means to keep people from seeking God.

Some argue that aspects of modern culture—such as the obsession with materialism, self-indulgence, and moral relativism—serve as tools of deception. For example, music, movies, social media, and other forms of entertainment, while not inherently evil, can sometimes propagate messages that conflict with godly principles. This does not mean that all human creativity is evil, but rather that Satan can manipulate human desires to lead people away from truth.

Understanding Different Religious Perspectives

While Christianity places great emphasis on the battle between God and Satan, other religions also acknowledge the presence of evil and spiritual opposition, though they may frame it differently. Understanding these perspectives can enrich our view of how different faith traditions interpret the struggle between good and evil.

Judaism

In Jewish thought, Satan (Ha-Satan) is not necessarily viewed as an independent force of evil in direct opposition to God. Instead, he is often seen as an accuser or adversary within the divine court, serving a role in testing and challenging human beings. The story of Job is an example where Satan is depicted as presenting challenges to test human faithfulness to God.

Islam

In Islam, Satan is known as Shaytan or Iblis, a being created from fire who refused to bow to Adam and was cast out of God's grace. Islamic teachings emphasize that Shaytan's mission is to lead humanity astray, whispering doubts and temptations. However, Islam also teaches that human beings have free will and can resist Shaytan through faith, prayer, and obedience to God (Allah). The Quran frequently warns against his deceptions and encourages believers to seek refuge in Allah from his influence.

Hinduism

Hinduism does not have a direct equivalent of Satan but recognizes powerful demonic forces known as Asuras that oppose the divine order. The struggle between good and evil is often depicted through epic battles in Hindu scriptures, such as in the Ramayana and Mahabharata. Concepts like Karma and Dharma (righteousness) play a crucial role in determining one's spiritual fate, with evil often being a product of ignorance and attachment rather than a singular, malevolent entity.

Buddhism

Buddhism speaks of Mara, a being who represents temptation and distraction from the path to enlightenment. Mara is often depicted as trying to prevent the Buddha from achieving Nirvana by presenting illusions and worldly desires. However, in Buddhism, the ultimate battle is against ignorance, attachment, and suffering, rather than a personified evil entity.

The Importance of Personal Faith and Free Will

One of the greatest gifts given to humanity is free will—the ability to choose between good and evil. Christianity teaches that while Satan may have influence over the world, he does not have ultimate power over individuals who choose to follow God.

It is important to recognize that religion and faith are deeply personal matters. People across cultures and religions seek spiritual fulfillment in different ways. While Christians believe that salvation comes through Jesus Christ, others find their paths through different means. Respect for differing beliefs does not mean compromising one's faith but rather understanding that the search for divine truth is a fundamental human pursuit.

The Role of Government and Religious Freedom

Throughout history, governments have played a role in either supporting or suppressing religious beliefs. In many Western nations, religious freedom is protected, allowing individuals to worship according to their convictions. However, in other parts of the world, religious persecution is a reality, particularly in totalitarian regimes or states where religious law governs society.

For example, communist governments have historically suppressed religion, seeing it as a threat to state authority. Islamic theocracies, on the other hand, enforce religious laws that dictate daily life. The balance between religious freedom and state control varies worldwide, affecting how people practice their faith.

The Ultimate Choice

As human beings, we all face the fundamental question: What is the purpose of life, and what happens after death? For Christians, the answer lies in Jesus Christ, who provides the way to eternal life. For others, the answers may be found in different religious traditions or philosophical understandings.

Regardless of one's beliefs, the awareness of mortality often brings spiritual reflection. Many people begin to seek deeper truths as they age, realizing that material pursuits are temporary. The fear of eternal separation from God—or, in other traditions, the cycle of suffering and rebirth—leads people to seek ways to attain spiritual peace.

Conclusion

The question of who rules this world is a profound one. While Christianity teaches that Satan has dominion over worldly affairs, it also assures believers that his power is limited. The ultimate victory belongs to God, and those who seek Him will find eternal life.

At the same time, understanding other religious perspectives helps foster a greater appreciation for the universal struggle between good and evil. Every faith tradition grapples with questions of morality, purpose, and the afterlife, emphasizing the need for individuals to seek truth with sincerity.

Faith, ultimately, is a deeply personal journey. Whether through Christianity, Islam, Judaism, Hinduism, Buddhism, or other belief systems, the search for spiritual truth remains one of the most significant aspects of human existence.

Chapter 5
About Demons

Demons seem to be everywhere, lurking in the shadows of our world and sometimes even within ourselves. It is as if they are an ever-present force, whispering through the corridors of time, weaving themselves into the fabric of existence. There are forces in the universe that oppose everything we know. Opposing energies are locked in an eternal battle. Life struggles against death. Good wrestles with evil. Matter clashes with antimatter. And demons are the unseen puppeteers of chaos, the malevolent architects of destruction, slipping into the minds and souls of the unsuspecting, often without their victims ever realizing they have been taken.

From the beginning, the natural world has been divided into the hunted and the hunters, the vulnerable and the predatory. Look at the great plains where herds of grazing animals live in fear of the fanged shadows that lurk in the tall grass. This same division existed even in the prehistoric world. Dinosaurs were locked in brutal battles, some struggling to survive while others sought only to kill. This duality echoes throughout history, woven into the stories of men and empires, into the very nature of human existence.

History tells of conquerors and warlords, men who were driven by an unrelenting force. Forces that did not originate from them alone but seemed to flow through them like an infernal river. Attila the Hun left cities smoldering in his wake, his brutal conquests fueled by something beyond mere ambition. Alexander the Great, brilliant yet relentless, marched through the known world as if an unseen hand guided his every step toward war and destruction. The kings of Babylon built their empire on the backs of the conquered, their cruelty knowing no bounds. The rulers of the Media Persian empire, with their thirst for dominance, bent entire civilizations to their will. And then, in more recent history, came those whose names are forever etched in infamy. Figures like the German Kaiser and Adolf Hitler, men who led millions into death and suffering, their eyes void of mercy, their souls seemingly lost to something dark and insatiable. Were they merely men, or were they vessels for something far more sinister?

It is a terrifying thought, the idea that anyone at any time might unknowingly fall under the influence of such darkness. A single moment of weakness, a crack in the armor of the soul, is all it takes for the unseen to enter, twisting thoughts and warping actions. A kind man may suddenly feel a terrible rage. A gentle soul may become a storm of destruction. We all walk a fine line, doing our best to live by the values instilled in us by our parents or guardians. But what happens when we let our guard down? When we entertain the whisper in the back of our minds that urges us toward malice, cruelty, or despair? The door opens. And once it does, the demon steps in.

Where all of this is leading, I do not know. What is the ultimate end of this battle, this endless conflict between forces that have existed since the dawn of time? Perhaps we are merely pawns, caught in a game beyond our understanding. Perhaps the war is not only external but also within us, and every choice we make is a battle in itself. What I do know is that the forces of darkness are real. They are watching, waiting for their moment to strike.

There are moments when the will to resist this force simply is not there. It weakens, crumbles, or is overwhelmed entirely. In those moments, a person can slip into a darkness so consuming that there is no return. The path to destruction is subtle at first. A fleeting thought of resentment toward another human being, barely noticeable and a passing shadow, can be the first whisper of something far more sinister. That seed of dislike, so small and seemingly insignificant, can take root and fester, growing into something monstrous. It is in those moments, when hatred stirs in the heart, that a demonic force finds its opening. The thought of harm becomes a possibility, then a desire, and finally, an action.

I have seen things that defy explanation. I have watched men and women perform acts beyond the realm of human ability, feats that should not be possible yet are. I have stood in a crowd as a magician manipulated reality before my eyes, bending the laws of nature as if they were mere suggestions. Some call it an illusion. I call it something else. There is a presence behind these things, something unseen yet undeniable. It lingers in the space between what we understand and what we fear.

Perhaps I sound like a pessimist. Maybe I am. I have a tendency to see the shadows where others see the light. But how can one witness the impossible and dismiss it as a mere trick? How can a person watch events unfold that should not, by any natural law, be happening and simply shrug them off? No, there is more at work in this world than we are led to believe. Forces beyond comprehension move among us, influencing, manipulating, and controlling.

And then there is time, or rather, the illusion of it. The past, the present, the future, it is all one. A great expanse without edges or boundaries. The human mind cannot grasp this, and yet, when I see images captured by the Hubble Space Telescope, when I look upon galaxies so distant that their light has traveled billions of years to reach us, I feel it. We are nothing but dust in an endless void. David, King of Israel, once wrote that mankind is so insignificant that we do not even tip the scales. We are weightless in the great balance of the universe. And yet, for all our smallness, we are also greater than the highest mountains because we are alive and because we are aware.

Sometimes I have the unsettling thought that everything around me, every person, every event, every twist of fate, exists only for me, as if I am the center of some cosmic illusion. It is a terrifying paradox to feel at once like the most important piece of the universe and yet completely powerless within it. Life tosses us about like leaves caught in a storm, dragging us along with no regard for our desires or fears. We are adrift in an endless ocean, struggling to stay afloat, and in the depths below, forces we cannot see stir in the darkness, waiting.

**

Chapter 6
My Prayer

A prayer to God Almighty should be more than mere words. It should be a pouring out of the soul, an offering of the deepest parts of ourselves to the One who already knows us better than we know ourselves. But to whom do we send this prayer? To the Creator of all things, the One who spoke the universe into existence, the One who holds the heavens in His hands and yet, despite His infinite power, listens to the smallest, most broken voice that dares to call out to Him.

And what do we have to offer Him, we who are but dust in the vastness of His creation? Nothing. No riches, no deeds, no sacrifices of our own making can add to His glory. He does not seek gifts of gold or offerings of grandeur, for everything already belongs to Him. The only thing He desires is our transformation, a reshaping of ourselves into a soul that is worthy to stand in His presence when the time of our passing comes. Yet how could I, who have stumbled through a life of sin and unbelief, ever hope to reach such a state? The weight of my failings is heavy upon me, and I have seen with painful clarity my inability to please my Maker.

But there is a miracle, a light that shines even in the darkest recesses of the soul. The Christ figure, the very Son of God, entered this world for the sake of those like me, those who have lost their way, those who have fallen again and again and are too weak to rise on their own. His coming was not one of earthly triumph, not the arrival of a mighty king seated upon a golden throne. No, He came in humility, born into a world that would reject Him, living a life of suffering and sorrow. He walked among the people, healing their sick, giving sight to the blind, restoring the broken, and yet even in the face of such undeniable miracles, unbelief thrived. Those who saw with their own eyes turned away, their hearts hardened, their minds clouded by doubt and pride.

And so I ask myself, how dare I even speak to God? How can one so lowly, so undeserving, lift their voice to the Almighty? As King David wrote so long ago, we are a speck of dust upon a scale, so insignificant in the grand design of the universe that our weight does not even register. Yet the truth is deeper than what the eye can see. For within us, beneath the flesh that will wither and return to the earth, there is something eternal. The spirit within us, the soul that gives us life, is what matters. And it is this soul that must be made pure, for it cannot stand in the presence of God if it remains stained by the sins of this world.

God does not seek perfection, for He alone is perfect. He does not demand that we be without flaws from the beginning but that we strive, that we fall and rise again, and that we seek Him even in our brokenness. Before we were born, our souls existed in His presence, untouched by the corruption of this world. But we were sent here, given this life to walk through, not as a meaningless journey but as a trial, a refining fire through which we must pass. Just as Christ walked the path of suffering, so too must we. Just as He faced temptation, so must we. And just as He overcame, so too must we strive to do the same.

This world is not an easy place, and the ruler of it seeks to lead us astray. He whispers in the shadows, tempts with empty promises, and lures with illusions of pleasure and power. Many are deceived. Many fall into his snare, their hearts hardened, their spirits dulled. But those who endure, those who refuse to be waylaid, those who hold steadfast to the truth, they will come to understand the purpose of it all. They will see that this life is not meant to break us but to shape us, to cleanse us of all that is unworthy, to prepare us for the Kingdom of Heaven.

And so I lift my prayer not with pride, not with confidence in my own worth, but with humility, knowing that I am nothing on my own. Yet through Him, I can be made whole. Through Him, I can be transformed. Through Him, I can stand before my Creator, not as one who is unworthy, but as one who has been redeemed.

Chapter 7
The King or Ruler of This World

Who truly rules this world? The answer is clear. Christ himself spoke of this ruler in the New Testament, stating that the ruler of this world had nothing to do with Him. The reason for this is that he knew Christ had come to overthrow his dominion, to break the chains that held humanity captive, and to offer a path to true freedom. There should be no misunderstanding about this. Satan and his legion of fallen angels are the real forces at work behind the corruption and deception that plague the world.

From the very beginning, Satan was present in the Garden of Eden. He appeared in the form of a serpent, cunningly deceiving the first humans, Adam and Eve, leading them to rebel against their Creator. He lured them into believing his lies, planting seeds of doubt and pride. As a result, humanity fell into sin. This tragic event severed the perfect relationship between mankind and God, introducing death, suffering, and the loss of eternal life. From that moment on, humanity was trapped under Satan's influence, unable to break free on its own.

However, God, in His mercy, had already prepared a way of salvation. The coming of Christ, the Messiah, and Redeemer, was the only means by which mankind could be rescued from eternal condemnation. Christ's sacrifice was the key to breaking the hold of Satan and providing a way for people to escape the grip of sin and reclaim the hope of eternal life. Yet, the battle for human souls continues. Satan, being one of the most intelligent and deceptive beings in existence, has not ceased his efforts to keep people blinded to the truth.

Through him, countless distractions have been introduced into the world. He is behind the many forms of entertainment, the endless pursuits of pleasure, the allure of power, and even the technological advancements that shape the way people think. He manipulates music, media, and ideologies to subtly draw people away from seeking God, using every possible avenue to keep their minds occupied with everything but the truth. The airwaves are filled with voices that drown out the message of salvation, leading people further into spiritual complacency.

Most of us go through life without truly understanding the weight of these realities until we reach a certain point. As we grow older, we begin to recognize our own mortality. The realization that life on this earth is temporary begins to settle in, and the haunting awareness of what lies beyond comes. The fear of eternal separation from God and the dread of damnation become more and more pressing. In those moments, many start to seek answers, to wonder if there is more to life than what this world offers.

But the good news remains. There is a way out. Christ's sacrifice was not in vain. He came so that those who believed in Him would not perish but have eternal life. The choice remains in the hands of each individual to continue living under the rule of the deceiver or to turn to the One who offers true and everlasting freedom.

I have realized that there are countless religions in the world today, each claiming to hold the ultimate truth about life, death, and the path to eternal existence. People follow their chosen beliefs with devotion, shaping their lives according to their respective faiths' teachings, customs, and doctrines. This is what we call freedom of religion, a principle that allows individuals to worship as they see fit without interference from governing authorities. In democratic societies, this freedom is protected, ensuring that people can seek and express their faith without fear of persecution. However, in totalitarian regimes, such as communist states or Islamic nations governed strictly by religious law, this freedom is often suppressed, and people may be forced to adhere to a particular belief system whether they accept it or not.

For those of us who live in what is commonly referred to as the Western world, Christianity remains the dominant faith. With Christianity comes the Bible, a sacred text that serves as millions' belief foundation. Though deeply rooted in Jewish tradition, the Bible is divided into two major sections: the Old Testament, which aligns with the Hebrew scriptures, and the New Testament, which introduces the teachings of Jesus Christ and is not recognized as part of the Jewish faith. For many in the Western world, the Bible is seen as the ultimate guide to eternal life, providing wisdom, instruction, and the promise of salvation through Christ.

Over time, I have come to understand that religion, at its core, is deeply personal. A person's relationship with God is something unique to them, shaped by their experiences, faith, and convictions. It should not be mocked, ridiculed, or dismissed simply because it differs from another's beliefs. Respecting someone's faith, even if we do not share it, is a sign of understanding and maturity. Everyone is on their own spiritual journey, searching for meaning and truth in their own way.

These are simply my thoughts, written down for anyone who wishes to read them. Whether one agrees or disagrees is entirely up to them, but I believe it is important to express what is in my heart. With that, I will bring this to a close, knowing that my reflections are now out in the open for others to consider.

Chapter 8
This World and its People

What can truly be said about this world, its people, and its purpose? This question has been asked for centuries, and countless books have been written attempting to explain how we, as human beings, came into existence. Some seek answers in science, while others turn to faith, and many find themselves somewhere in between.

I find the concept of the Big Bang to be the most compelling explanation for the universe's origins. Whether one believes in a divine Creator who set everything in motion or prefers a purely scientific perspective, the idea remains that a single, powerful event led to the formation of everything we see today. This cosmic explosion formed stars, galaxies, and planets, creating the vast universe we now observe.

When it comes to the question of life itself, there are two main schools of thought that attempt to explain how living beings came into existence. One perspective is rooted in the idea that life began as a single microscopic cell that somehow came to be, perhaps through a unique combination of elements and conditions that allowed it to form. Through an extraordinary process, this simple cell managed to reproduce itself, setting off a chain reaction that would eventually lead to the diversity of life on Earth. Some believe that this process was purely natural, driven by the forces of evolution, while others suggest that a guiding intelligence may have played a role.

According to this theory, the first signs of life emerged in the form of primitive single-celled organisms, such as algae, which eventually gave rise to more complex plant life. Over time, simple forms of vegetation evolved into grass, shrubs, and trees, gradually shaping the planet into the lush and diverse world we know today. This incredible progression, from a single cell to an entire ecosystem of flora, is often described as one of the greatest mysteries of existence.

No matter which explanation one chooses to believe, the origins of life remain one of the most fascinating topics of human inquiry. Whether life was the result of divine intervention, the inevitable outcome of natural laws, or a combination of both, the search for meaning continues. We may never have all the answers, but the journey of discovery itself is what makes life so remarkable.

The other perspective is the belief in a Creator who is all-powerful, all-knowing, and capable of bringing something into existence from nothing. According to this view, the Big Bang was not a random event but rather the deliberate act of a divine being setting everything in motion. If such an entity has the ability to create entire galaxies, including our own Milky Way, then it would not be difficult to believe that this same force could also shape and sustain the universe over time. The vastness and complexity of the cosmos, from the intricate structure of atoms to the immense scale of galaxies, point to a level of intelligence and design beyond human comprehension.

One of the most well-known accounts of creation is found in the Christian Bible, where it is written that God created the heavens and the earth in seven days. Many people take this description literally, believing that the universe and everything in it came into being within a single week. However, I personally do not interpret these "days" in a strict 24-hour sense. The Bible itself states that one day to God is like a thousand years, or even longer, possibly stretching into millions of years. If we consider this perspective, the creation story aligns more closely with what we understand about the formation of the universe and the Earth.

Following the biblical narrative, the early Earth would have started as a molten mass, filled with intense heat and swirling with elements that would eventually form the planet's structure. During this period, the young Earth was likely surrounded by a dense, smoke-filled atmosphere, making it impossible to see the newly formed sun. Over an immense span of time, perhaps millions of years, the planet would have gradually cooled, allowing the thick clouds of smoke and gas to dissipate. Eventually, as the atmosphere cleared, the sun's light would have reached the Earth's surface, marking a crucial step in the development of a world capable of supporting life.

Whether one believes in a purely scientific explanation or a divinely guided process, the origins of the universe and our planet remain an incredible mystery. The idea that everything we see today—from the vast galaxies to the smallest living organisms—began from a single explosion of energy or the spoken command of a Creator continues to spark deep thought, discussion, and debate. While we may never fully grasp the ultimate truth behind creation, exploring these possibilities allows us to appreciate the wonder and complexity of existence itself.

There is significant evidence that during Earth's cooling period, it was bombarded by meteors and asteroids, many of which were composed of solid ice. As these ice-laden celestial bodies crashed into the planet, they melted upon impact, gradually forming vast oceans, lakes, and rivers. This influx of water also contributed to the formation of thick steam clouds that enveloped the Earth, creating an atmosphere that further cooled the planet by blocking and diffusing the sun's intense heat. Over an extended period, this cooling process stabilized, setting the stage for the next phases of Earth's transformation.

According to the biblical creation account, it is said that God's spirit hovered over the waters, and soon after, vegetation began to emerge. Lush plant life, including grasses, shrubs, and towering trees, took root and spread across the land. This process, rather than occurring instantly, likely unfolded over an immense span of time—perhaps another million years or more. As the Earth's atmosphere continued to clear, the sky became visible, and the sun, moon, and stars could be seen in their full brilliance, marking another significant shift in Earth's development.

With the foundation of life set, the life-giving force now turned toward the creation of living creatures. The oceans and seas became filled with vast marine life, from the smallest microscopic organisms to massive sea creatures. Birds of all kinds took to the skies, adapting to the world around them. This period, too, may have lasted for another million years as life in the waters and air continued to flourish and evolve.

At the same time, the land began to teem with creatures of all shapes and sizes. From insects to wild animals to domesticated creatures such as cattle, every species that would ever walk the Earth was introduced in its time. Among these ancient inhabitants were the mighty dinosaurs, ruling the land in all their splendor. However, it is my belief that while they thrived for a time, they were not meant to coexist with humanity. Whether through natural disasters, climate shifts, or other catastrophic events, they were ultimately removed from the equation before mankind entered the scene.

This grand process of creation, whether viewed through a lens of faith, science, or a combination of both, speaks to the immense complexity and order of the universe. Each stage prepared the way for the next, culminating in a world perfectly suited for the arrival of humankind. While the precise details may forever remain a mystery, the evidence of a vast and carefully woven history is undeniable, leaving us to wonder at the intricate forces that shaped the world we now call home.

If a divine entity, a God-like being, had the power to create the vast universe with all its galaxies, stars, and planets, then how difficult would it be for that same Creator to form a man and a woman in His own image and sustain them through the ages? The very existence of life, with all its intricacies and wonders, suggests a design far beyond human comprehension. The purpose behind the creation of mankind is a subject of great depth, and as promised, I will now share my thoughts on it.

According to the biblical account, the Trinity—Father, Son, and Holy Spirit—made the decision to create humankind in their own image. The Earth, which had undergone an incredible transformation over millions of years, was now ready to support life, and so the first man, Adam, was formed. Shortly after, Eve was created to be his companion, and together, they were placed in a magnificent paradise, a place of perfect harmony where they could live without suffering, toil, or death. From these first two human beings, all of mankind eventually came into existence.

Genesis tells us that Adam and Eve were given freedom and dominion over all creation, but there was one command they were expected to obey. They were forbidden from eating the fruit of a specific tree, known as the Tree of the Knowledge of Good and Evil. This was a test of their trust and obedience to their Creator. However, despite the perfection of their surroundings, the temptation proved too strong. In an act of disobedience, they ate the forbidden fruit and, in doing so, brought sin into the world.

This single act of defiance had profound consequences for Adam and Eve and all of humanity. They were cast out of Paradise and forced to live in a world that was now filled with hardship, pain, and mortality. While they had originally been created to live eternally, their disobedience introduced death into the human experience. In the early generations, people still lived to extraordinary ages, but over time, lifespans shortened, and death became an inevitable part of existence.

This moment in history marked a turning point for mankind. It was no longer a world of pure perfection but one where suffering and struggle became part of life. However, the story does not end there. The Bible also speaks of redemption and hope, a plan set in motion to restore what was lost. This is a subject that I will expand upon in due time, but for now, it is important to reflect on the origins of humanity and the choices that shaped our world.

When mankind was created, human beings were given a living soul, something that would exist beyond their physical bodies and continue even after death. This soul is what sets humanity apart from other forms of life, as it is not merely a temporary breath but an eternal aspect of our being. According to biblical teaching, the creation of mankind was not just about populating the earth but was part of a larger divine purpose. Humanity was given the ability to think, choose, and seek a relationship with its Creator.

God, in His knowledge of all things, foresaw what would unfold in the history of mankind. According to scripture, He had a plan from the beginning. This plan involved allowing human beings to exercise free will and make their own decisions while also having the opportunity to choose righteousness. The Bible teaches that God desires people to live by His will, and those who remain faithful to Him will one day be in His presence.

To understand this plan more fully, it is necessary to look at what Scripture says about events that took place before the creation of mankind. The Bible speaks of a time when a great number of angels served God. Among them was one who became proud and sought to elevate himself above all others. This angel, later referred to as Satan, refused to submit to God's authority and led a rebellion. As a result, he and those who followed him were cast out of their original position and were no longer part of God's divine order.

Scripture describes Satan as being present in the world, exerting influence over people and leading them away from the truth. Alongside him are those who joined him in rebellion, and they continue to promote deception and opposition to God's ways. The Bible teaches that mankind has been placed in a position to choose whom they will serve, whether it be the truth of God or the falsehoods introduced by Satan.

From a biblical perspective, this is the central purpose of human existence. Everyone is allowed to seek God and live according to His will. Those who do so are promised eternal life in His presence. While mankind was originally created to live in perfect harmony with God, disobedience led to separation. However, scripture also teaches that this separation can be restored through faith and obedience.

The world as we see it today reflects this ongoing reality. People hold different beliefs, seek different ways to understand existence and make different choices regarding faith and morality. The Bible presents a clear path for those who desire to know the truth, offering guidance on how to live a life that is in alignment with God's purpose. In the end, each person must decide which path they will follow.

Here on Earth, Satan and his followers are actively influencing many aspects of the world's affairs by working through the minds of those who are vulnerable to deception. They entice, tempt, and lead people into wrongdoing, especially those who are already inclined toward selfishness, greed, or immoral behavior. The forces of evil thrive wherever people allow themselves to be guided by their own desires rather than by God's truth. The temptation to stray from what is right is always present, and resisting it requires constant vigilance.

The only way to stand against these influences is by remaining on guard and following the teachings found in the Bible. Scripture provides clear instructions on how to live a righteous life, resist temptation, and stay connected to God. It serves as a guide that helps believers navigate a world filled with deception, offering wisdom and strength to overcome the challenges that come with spiritual warfare.

God, in His infinite wisdom, knew from the very beginning that humanity would face these struggles. He understood that people would be tempted, that sin would enter the world, and that many would turn away from Him. Because of this, He made a way for mankind to be redeemed. This plan involved sending His Son, Jesus Christ, to Earth to serve as a sacrifice for those who choose to accept Him as their Savior. Through His sacrifice, those who follow Him can be forgiven and restored to a right relationship with God.

By accepting Christ and obeying God's commandments, believers have the opportunity to secure eternal life with Him. This is not just about avoiding punishment but about being transformed into the people God intended us to be. It is about growing in faith, living a life of righteousness, and ultimately being welcomed into God's presence for eternity. Our souls are not meant to perish but to live forever, and through God's plan of salvation, He offers each person the chance to be with Him in heaven.

Chapter 9
The Sea of Mankind

When I look over the sea of mankind, I see the remnants of a world that once was. A world where kindness and respect shaped the way people interacted. A world where conversations were meaningful and human connection was valued above self-interest. Those ways have faded, slipping away like whispers on the wind, replaced by a society that prioritizes speed, convenience, and personal gain. The question is no longer: *How can I help you?* But rather, *What can you do for me today?*

With modernization comes a paradox. We are more connected than ever, yet more distant than before. News from the farthest corners of the world reaches us in seconds, but real conversations have grown shallow. Families sit together yet remain apart, their eyes fixed on screens instead of one another. Parents struggle to understand a generation raised by algorithms and instant gratification, feeling lost as their children become strangers in their own homes.

Beyond the walls of our daily lives, the world itself trembles under the weight of its own conflicts. Entire populations are being driven from their homes, forced to flee from the grip of extremism and violence. The thirst for power has overshadowed the value of life, and ideological battles are waged not with reason but with bloodshed. We watch helplessly as humanity inches toward a breaking point, one that threatens to unravel the fragile threads holding our world together.

A great storm is coming, one that will not be confined to a single nation or people. It will touch every corner of the earth, leaving no one unaffected. The weapons of war, once the subject of nightmares, may soon become reality. When that time arrives, there will be no neutral ground. Every person will be forced to choose a side, not by choice but by the circumstances that surround them.

What troubles me most is not just the conflict itself but the fear and uncertainty that will consume us before it even begins. The unknown will loom over us like a shadow, and those with children will feel the weight of it the most. The desperate search for safety will become all-consuming, but the hardest truth to accept will be that nowhere is truly safe.

It gives me no pleasure to write these words, yet something within me compels me to do so. It is as if this urgency, this unshakable feeling, must be expressed before it fades away into silence. To write is to release the burden. To remain silent is to let it die within me, unheard and forgotten.

And so, for now, I write.

Chapter 10
Past Sense

When I look back on the times gone by

And feel the emotions again of the past,

I wonder whatever possessed me to wander

On the path that led me to this sorry state.

I know that to see me, you hardly do notice.

The aches that so torment my heart for so long,

But go on, I must, as time does some healing,

Although ever so slowly, as memories last.

Who knows what the future will bring to us all?

The hopes and the fears, whatever befall us.

What is it that plays on our mind and our soul,

To keep us going in this circle again and again?

I know they all say, "Don't live in the past."

Look forward and enter a new way of life

That will make you happy and not sad.

It is easy to say for those not in my shoes.

At ease with myself, I must become,

On the gentle waves of my thoughts,

The blue skies that hover over my soul,

Trying to dispel the gathering clouds of fear.

Religion creeps in and gives me thoughts to ponder.

What path to take, instead of laying down in slumber?

Wake up, I must, as time goes by so speedily.

Get hold of the truth, which always sets one free.

I wrote this down to speak to myself and ponder

What is inside of me and to impart to others

That no one is alone and no one is an island.

No matter what, it's only love that can cure all

Chapter 11
More Thoughts and Angst

It's not easy to admit to yourself, *"Woe is me."* It's hard to face the truth of what we've done, especially when we know that one day, we'll have to stand before God and give an account of our lives. I know this deeply in my heart. And yet, I still struggle to truly accept that God could forgive someone like me. I feel like I sin more with every passing day, and the weight of those sins feels heavier and heavier on my shoulders.

My wrongs aren't just small mistakes. They include the way I've hurt my own family, the ones who should have been safest with me. I've also failed the people who put their trust in me. The list of my failures is long, and I can't make excuses anymore. I have no one to blame but myself. And that truth haunts me.

I'm terrified of that final day when all the people I've hurt might look at me with pain in their eyes and point their fingers in judgment. I fear they'll cry out against me, confirming what I already know—that I deserve nothing less than hell for the way I've lived. I have spoken words I should never have spoken and lived too often, thinking only of myself.

What cuts even deeper is that I've spent years studying faith, talking about God, and even writing books on spiritual truths. I should know better. I *do* know better. But knowledge without obedience means nothing. When the time comes to face my Maker, what will I say? How could I explain all this? The shame I carry is so deep, and "I'm sorry" feels like too small a phrase. Even if I gave my life to save another, it would not erase the damage I've done, especially to those closest to me.

I look around and see others living better lives than me, even those who don't claim to know much about God. I feel like the worst of them all. The guilt is so strong. Oh God, how I need Your mercy. How I long for the kind of forgiveness that only You can give—the kind that Jesus offers, the kind that covers even the darkest parts of us and washes them clean.

Jesus, where are You? Why do I feel so far from You now? Why do You seem so silent? I am lost and lonely. I feel cut off from everything good and holy. Please, Lord, come to me, even in the quiet of the night. Speak to me. Help me see what I've been blind to for so long. Soften my heart. Open my eyes before it's too late before my time here is over, and I lie down for the last time.

Like the apostle Paul said, "I know what I *should* do, but I don't do it." And the very things I know I *shouldn't* do, I end up doing again and again. Who will rescue me from this life that feels like death? Only You, Jesus. Only You.

As we grow older, the dreams of greatness and the grand plans we once had start to fade away. The things that once felt so important and full of promise slowly lose their shine. The fire we once had, the drive that pushed us to do more, to be more, begins to dim little by little. At first, we don't notice it. We go about our daily lives, caught up in the routine, and we don't realize how much energy we've lost until we stop, even for just a moment, and reflect. It's in those quiet moments of reflection that we see the truth: we can no longer live with the same intensity we once did.

And yet, in that moment of realization, there's often a sudden burst of energy. It's like a flash of clarity when we open our eyes wide and remember the dreams, the hopes, and the passions we once had. For a brief time, we feel like we're back on track, moving forward with purpose, seeing both where we've been and where we might still go. But as time marches on, those bursts of energy become less frequent. The lapses come again, and we find ourselves weak, vulnerable, and fragile. It's as if the smallest obstacle or breeze can slow us down, sometimes even bringing us to a halt.

I realize, as I write these words, that this experience is not true for everyone. There are people who seem to have endless energy and continue to live with vigor and purpose until their last breath. They seem untouched by time, continuing to move through life with a strength that defies age. But for me, it's different. I'm not like others, and in that, I suppose I am unique. Each of us is, in our own way, a reflection of our own journey—a journey that's different from anyone else's. There is no one exactly like me, nor is there likely to be, by the grace of God.

And while I may not have the same energy I once did, I am learning to accept that this is simply part of my path. It's part of growing older, and in its own way, it carries its own kind of beauty. It's a reminder to cherish what we have in the present, to be thankful for the moments we still have, and to recognize that even in our frailty, there's still a unique purpose that only we can fulfill.

Chapter 12
Here and Now

Here I am, in this moment, sitting quietly and reflecting on my past. I can't seem to get beyond the present. The past is just there, like a faint memory that sometimes feels distant, almost unreachable. I know my past isn't as exciting or glamorous as others. I didn't have those clear goals, the drive to achieve them, or the success stories that some people can boast about. I didn't excel in sports, and there were no family vacations or trips to places far away because we simply couldn't afford them. My life was simple, sheltered in its own way. But here I am, still breathing, still standing. Despite everything, I'm alive, and that's something to be thankful for.

So now, what's next? What comes after this moment of reflection? Should I keep going, or is this all there is? The world around me is filled with people who have led such interesting, colorful lives. Their stories are often captivating, full of excitement, adventure, and daring decisions. Sometimes, I wish I could be more like them, but the truth is, I am who I am. My life hasn't been filled with grand stories, and I think the ones I have might seem boring to most. Maybe they are. But they are mine, and that has to be enough.

The one thing I feel sets me apart, even if just a little, is my understanding of the Bible. I was raised in a religious family, where my father was the head of the household, and we were expected to follow his lead. It wasn't always easy, but those years shaped me in a way that gave me a perspective on faith that others might not have. But now, we're all grown, free to make our own decisions. And with that freedom, I've come to realize just how overwhelming it can be to be an adult.

Becoming an adult means taking on so many responsibilities, each one weighing on your shoulders. The choices we make every day can change the course of our lives in ways we may not fully understand. A single decision, a choice we make in the course of a year, can have ripple effects that last a lifetime. It makes me think about the path we take in life. How many times have we heard of the "road not taken"? Sometimes, I wonder if I chose the right one. Sometimes, I don't even know what the right choice is.

One thing that often occupies my thoughts is the question of what is good and what is evil. Good is easy to understand, but what about evil? What truly is evil? When I think about the animal world, it's clear that survival is a constant battle. Predators hunt and kill because they need to eat; they do it for survival, just like any other creature in nature. It's part of the cycle of life, even if it seems cruel. But in human society, it's not so simple. When I look at history, at the atrocities committed in the name of power, whether it's by a king, an emperor, or a dictator, I feel my heart ache. I wonder how this happens. Why do we let these things happen? What drives people to commit such horrors in the name of something greater than themselves?

I think about all the young men who have gone off to war, fighting for their countries, their empires, or their kings. They march into battle, believing they are fighting for a cause that is noble, only to die in the end, often for nothing. So many of these empires and kingdoms have crumbled, leaving behind only dust and ruins. The people who gave their lives for these causes are mostly forgotten, and their sacrifices are barely remembered. They're just names in history books, their stories lost to time.

And now, at this very moment, I think of what is happening in the world. The ISIS movement, for example, is causing unimaginable suffering. Entire populations are being displaced, fleeing for their lives. Families are torn apart, and millions of people are living in fear. The refugees are scattered across borders, searching for safety, but even that is elusive. Governments are overwhelmed, struggling to manage the crisis that continues to grow. The hardships these people face are beyond words, and it's hard to comprehend the scale of the pain they are enduring. It's a stark reminder of the evil that still exists in the world and the way hatred and violence can destroy so many lives.

It all makes me question the nature of humanity. What drives us to do the things we do? Are we doomed to repeat the same mistakes over and over again? I wish I had the answers, but maybe, in the end, that's something we'll never fully understand. All we can do is try to make the world a little better, one decision at a time.

It is often said that when a poisonous snake is found, the only way to protect oneself is to cut off its head. This is a powerful metaphor for what is happening in the world today, especially in the Middle East. There is a war taking place that no one wants, but it continues to rage, and the consequences of ignoring it are devastating. The situation is spiraling into chaos, much like what we saw during the Second World War when millions of people were forced to flee their homes to escape violence and destruction. Families were torn apart, lives were lost, and entire generations were forever scarred.

Yet today, despite the suffering of countless innocent people, the Western world seems to stand by, doing very little to help. The United Nations, the League of Nations that came before it, and all the other international organizations seem to be watching from the sidelines, unable or unwilling to take meaningful action. Their silence is deafening as the world burns around them. Meanwhile, the makers of weapons are making enormous profits from the conflict. It doesn't matter to them who buys their weapons, whether they are used by tyrants or terrorists; as long as money keeps flowing into their pockets, they are satisfied.

This is the harsh reality of our world today. There seems to be no solution, but there is one. If only the world's leaders, the powers that be, would step in and put an end to the wars, the bloodshed, and the greed that is driving this destruction. It's hard to fathom that in this day and age, we still have to fight so hard for peace and justice. The world should not be this way. Yet, we are left watching helplessly, waiting for someone to take responsibility and make the hard choices that could stop the suffering.

We've seen what happens when leaders finally rise up and take a stand. It took more than five long years to defeat Hitler and his regime, but the world came together to end the evil that was sweeping across Europe. It was a long and painful journey, but it showed that when the international community acts with resolve, it can overcome even the most powerful forces of evil. If similar action were taken against the leaders who are causing so much destruction today, the cycle of violence could end. The oppression of countless people would cease, and peace could finally take root.

What the world needs now more than ever is unity. Imagine a world where Christians, Jews, Buddhists, Muslims, and all other faiths could live side by side in peace. A world where people respect one another, regardless of their differences, and work together for the common good. This may seem like an impossible dream, but if we don't strive for it, how can we ever hope to achieve it? The answer lies in action, real, meaningful action taken by those who have the power to make change. The fate of millions rests in their hands, and it is their responsibility to bring an end to the bloodshed, the suffering, and the greed that fuels these endless wars.

Chapter 13
Where am I

What unspeakable torment the soul endures, even when surrounded by familiar faces and places. There is a sense of being lost, though everything around you seems so familiar. It's a deep, aching confusion that consumes the mind. The pain of not knowing how to escape the feelings of disconnection, wanting desperately to grasp onto anything that can reassure you that you are not truly lost. You are not far from home, just overwhelmed—bewildered by something, an event, or a circumstance that perhaps you couldn't control. It could be the weight of an unexpected tragedy or the scars of past mistakes that were never fully healed. It doesn't matter how hard you try; it feels like nothing can ease the emptiness.

Friends look at you with knowing eyes, nodding in sympathy as if they understand. But deep down, you know they can never truly feel what you are going through. They mean well, but their comfort only seems to go skin deep. It's like they're just going through the motions of being supportive, yet they cannot reach the very depths of your despair. Past events, long buried, surge back with the force of a tidal wave. Every memory feels like a ghost from another life—one that feels as if it belonged to someone else in a time so distant that it's almost as if it never existed. Yet, like a cruel reminder, the memories return again and again, constantly reminding you of the things you wish you could forget.

They lurk, buried deep in the recesses of the mind. Despite all the distractions of life, despite the years that have passed, these thoughts seem to come out of nowhere, like a worm burrowing through layers of dirt and chaos. They emerge unexpectedly, often at the worst moments—when you're alone, when you're weak, or when life demands the most from you. It feels like an endless cycle, and no matter how much you try to push it away, it always comes back. It's hard to shake the feeling that you are somehow being held captive by these memories, trapped in a prison of your own making.

And the question remains: will we ever be free? Or are we destined to be chained forever by the events of the past, like prisoners with no hope of escape? It's a question that haunts many of us. I know not everyone lives with this constant weight. Some people seem to glide through life without being bogged down by the mistakes or regrets of their past, but most of us are not so fortunate. Who among us is truly perfect, without fault, without sin? We are all burdened in some way, whether we acknowledge it or not. For some, the pain is so deeply buried that it is as though it no longer affects them—like a conscience seared shut with a hot iron. For these people, it seems there is no hope of redemption, for they cannot even recognize their own wrongs, let alone feel the desire to change. Their hearts are hardened, and their souls are lost in ways that we cannot understand.

But for those of us who still feel the sting of regret, who wish for a way out of the prison of our own minds, there is hope. For us, there is a chance to heal, to be forgiven, to lay down the heavy burdens we carry. It may feel impossible, but there is always hope for change. And I know, as you can tell, my thoughts often turn to matters of faith, to the question of salvation and redemption. What else is there to turn to, really, when everything else seems temporary, fleeting, and unreliable?

I suppose a psychiatrist might be able to offer some help, and I'm sure their words could bring comfort or at least some guidance. But in the end, the cycle continues. The thoughts return. The doubts creep back in. And before long, we find ourselves stuck in the same place as before, struggling to move forward. We can only find true peace and true freedom by confronting the deepest issues of our soul—our need for forgiveness, our need to be redeemed from the weight of our sins.

The only way to be truly freed from the chains of guilt and regret is through the forgiveness of sins. And the only one who can offer this forgiveness, the only one who can truly heal our broken souls, is Jesus Christ. He is the answer to our deepest pain. Only through His grace and mercy can we hope to find the peace we desperately seek. For all the mistakes, all the hurt, all the shame that weighs us down—Jesus can take it from us. His love is the only way to set us free.

Chapter 14
More thoughts

When I listen to the songs sung by voices now silenced by time, voices of those who have long since departed this world, I feel an ache that settles deep within my chest. Their melodies drift through the air like distant memories, filled with echoes of laughter, hope, and dreams once dreamt. I see their young faces, once so full of life and wonder, captured in faded photographs or flickering film, and my heart grows heavy. A profound sadness rises in me, gentle yet overwhelming, and soon, a tear begins its quiet journey down my cheek. My eyes mist over as if trying to soften the sharp edge of realization that time carries with it.

In those quiet, aching moments, I came to understand how temporary everything truly is. The world moves on, but traces of those who came before linger like whispers on the wind. No matter how long it lasts, life feels so small when placed beside the age of the stars and the infinite stretch of the universe. Each of us is a traveler, walking the path that has been set before us, often without knowing the destination. We do our best, even when it feels like the weight of existence is too much to carry, even when the light is hard to find.

I have a deep longing that cannot be quieted to become one with everything, to feel a part of something far greater than this fleeting life. I want to understand the meaning behind it all, to know why we are here and what purpose our joy and pain truly serve. While we are here, we understand only in part as if looking through a fogged window. But I believe that a day will come when all will be made clear. On that day, everything will finally make sense, and we will witness the truth and become part of it, part of the great story we were always meant to join.

In that place of knowing, truth will rise like the sun after a long night and set us free. No longer lost in doubt or fear, we will stand in the fullness of what we were created to be. We will see not with human eyes but with understanding that goes beyond reason, beyond time. We will be part of God's eternal kingdom, united with Him who gave His only begotten Son, not sparing Him but offering Him out of boundless love. He gave Him to those who would crucify Him so that we might be redeemed and reclaimed as beloved children of the Father.

What are we, really, but dust gathered from the earth? Yet, within that dust, there is something powerful, something eternal. Though a mountain may rise higher, with all its strength and stillness, it knows nothing of love or grief. It cannot weep; it cannot hope. But we, made from earth and breath, can feel the fire of life within us. That fire gives us something no stone or star can hold: the ability to seek, remember, believe, and love. And in that, perhaps, lies the greatest truth of all.

Chapter 15
Listening

Here I am, sitting alone in the quiet of my room, with nothing but the soft glow of a lamp and the haunting sound of ancient psalms echoing gently from the speakers beside me. These sacred hymns, sung long ago by voices now long gone, seem to wrap around my soul like a warm, aching memory. Each note tugs at my heartstrings, pulling me back through time to days that live only in my memory now, days of innocence, laughter, and the comforting presence of those I loved most. I see us again, gathered around the table, my sisters laughing, my parents' eyes full of life and love. The world then felt whole.

But now, as the music washes over me, tears begin to slip quietly down my cheeks. They fall without shame because I feel something close to forsaken at this moment. The memories come not in faded fragments but in vivid, piercing waves. I can still hear the sound of my mother's voice, smell the warm bread from our kitchen, and feel the sun on my face as we played outside together. Time has moved on, but it has not dulled the edges of those recollections. It has made them sharper, more precious, and more painful.

There is a sorrow in me that words often fail to hold. A sorrow not only for the ones I've lost but also for the parts of myself I have failed, for choices I made that I cannot undo. Deep down, I carry this weight, knowing that some of what has come my way was not just fate but consequence. And still, the soul searches for understanding. The good Lord has not turned His face from me. Instead, He had visited me in moments when I least expected it. He has taught me lessons and carved them into the walls of my heart with a quiet, firm hand. Yet, while my heart often understands, my mind resists. It wrestles with the why of it all, searching for answers where none are given.

There are times when I acknowledge it all, from A to Z, yet something within me still tries to run, still seeks a way to escape, even when every door is shut tight. And so, I stand in silence, facing myself, forced to absorb the blame, whether I am ready to or not. In those moments, thoughts arise that try to comfort me. They whisper, "It's not so bad," and point fingers at those who have done far worse: tyrants, murderers, the architects of human suffering. But I know these are hollow comparisons. The soul is not measured by comparison but by truth. I know that we are each responsible for our own choices, and ultimately, we must each bear the consequences of what we have done or failed to do.

Even with this awareness, there has been grace. I could have been left to walk this life alone, condemned to solitude and regret. But God, in His mercy, reached into the dim corners of my life and placed someone there, a lifeline I did not earn, a soul who has walked with me and carried me when I could not walk on my own. I cannot begin to measure what they gave me or the debt I owe for their love and patience. It is a kind of mercy that leaves me speechless because I know I deserve none of it.

As the days pass more quickly and the calendar pages seem to turn of their own accord, I feel time pressing in. I glance through the obituary column and recognize more and more names. Some are older, some the same age as I am, and some heartbreakingly younger. It is a sober reminder that the end is no longer a distant thought but a train approaching with the speed and certainty of a freight engine. There is no stopping it. There is only the question of whether I am ready, have made peace, found gratitude, and clung to the light I've been given.

Thankfully, there is an escape, an extraordinary hope offered by the Savior of all mankind. It is a path not earned by works or wisdom but gifted by grace to those chosen to believe, to those whose hearts respond to the quiet call of the Redeemer. I hold onto this hope like a lifeline, though I often feel as if I am fumbling in the dark to understand it all. I have shelves lined with books, pages full of theology and prophecy, of doctrine and mystery. And yet, so few of them I have read. They sit there like unopened letters, waiting for a quieter season, a deeper clarity. But time is no longer stretching out in front of me as it once did. I can feel its wings beating faster now.

These days, I feel as if I am standing at the very threshold of eternity. My body is aging, my strength waning, and yet my soul grows more restless with each passing hour. It cries out to the One who has walked beside me all my life, even in the seasons when I didn't recognize His presence. There's a stirring in me, a blend of impatience and awe, fear and faith. I long to know what awaits me, not just in this moment but in the eternal one that follows.

Lately, I've heard whispers of disaster, predictions of a cosmic event that could shake the earth to its core. A mysterious planet, previously hidden from human sight, is said to be on a collision course with our orbit, threatening to disturb the balance of the skies. Some say this event will be unlike anything modern humanity has witnessed. That ocean will surge over the land, islands vanish, mountains crumble, and skies darken with ash and smoke. Entire cities may be erased as the world groans under the weight of cataclysm.

Is it true? I do not know. But it has stirred something deep in me, a question that won't be silenced: *Is there a way to survive the end of the world and the judgment that may come with it?*

I'm not trying to preach. I am no prophet, no authority, just a man reflecting on what could be the closing chapters of our story. But in the

Christian Scriptures, a promise shines brighter than any fear: the hope of the rapture. It speaks of a moment when those who believe in Christ, who have placed their faith in Him as Savior and Redeemer, will be caught up, and removed from the devastation to come. Some scoff at this idea, dismissing it as fantasy or delusion. But to me, it is a promise that whispers peace in a world filled with tremors.

Yes, this is a simplified version of the rebirth experience. I know that. But I felt compelled to write it down anyway. Because somewhere inside, beneath all the fear and confusion, there is a quiet clarity. If even a fraction of what is prophesied comes to pass, if the pole shifts and the earth is shaken as described by Velikovsky in *Earth in Upheaval*, then the planet as we know it will be changed forever. According to biblical prophecy, mountains will be tossed about like pebbles; volcanoes will erupt with apocalyptic fury; the seas will roar and cover the lowlands. The sun will shine no brighter than the light behind a veil of sackcloth, and the moon and stars will vanish from our view.

And then what? Who will survive? Who will be left to rebuild from the ashes?

I imagine people reading this might shake their heads and wonder, *What is he talking about?* And truthfully, I wonder, too. Who am I to write about these things? Why do I feel the need to put all this on paper? I don't have all the answers. I barely have the questions. But I know what my heart is whispering tonight.

These are my thoughts: fragile, honest, incomplete. Thoughts about the world's end, or perhaps just the end of my own journey in it. Either way, the urgency is the same. I do not know what tomorrow holds. None of us do. But I know that mercy exists, and it is not too late to reach out.

So may God have mercy on the world, the weary, and the children yet to see the light of day. May He shelter the souls who cry out for hope and lead us, trembling but willing, into His arms.

Chapter 16
My Cry

O God… I am so hopelessly lost, not just in this fleeting moment but in the vast expanse of time and space itself. The centuries seem to press down upon me like towering boulders, heavy with history and meaning I cannot decipher. I stumble beneath their weight, searching for a way through, yet finding none. The path is obscured by shadows of questions that have no answers. The lessons I've gathered along the way, those moments of clarity hard-won through pain and trial, feel small now, inadequate, like scattered pebbles before the cliffs of eternity.

I must confess what I've long hidden, even from myself. From early childhood, I never grasped the meaning of life. Not really. I lived, yes, but I did not *live fully*. I moved through time as one watching from behind a veil, letting days slip by like sand through open fingers. Time was wasted, squandered on trivial things, distractions that masked my deeper ache. What could have been filled with purpose and passion was instead muted by indecision and fear.

Yes, I wrote some books. I tried to explain myself, to give shape to the inner turmoil and the longing that has followed me like a shadow. But to what end? The words, while sincere, feel now like ripples on a vast sea. Did they touch anyone? Did they matter? Sometimes, I wonder if the expression "No man is an island" is, in fact, a comforting lie because I have often felt like one, adrift, isolated, disconnected from the stream of humanity that flows so confidently onward.

I find myself rambling, trying to give form to something that resists being named. The thoughts in my mind seem to slip away just as I reach for them as if they do not wish to be held. I long to follow the clear, bold lines drawn in the sands of history, the lines that defined greatness in men and in nations. But every time I gaze upon those lines, I realize how fragile they really are. Time is not kind. It reshapes and erases with cruel ease. What once stood tall and sure is eventually washed away, replaced by newer, louder ideologies.

Today, it seems that all the sacred values once held so dearly by our forebears, values of honor, discipline, humility, and reverence, have been cast aside. In their place, permissiveness reigns. We chase novelty over wisdom, indulgence over restraint. And in this cultural shift, entire nations lose their identity, their soul. We don't need to look far into the past to see the consequences. Germany, once a cradle of reform, of spiritual awakening through the voices of Calvin and Luther, descended into the abyss under the iron rule of Hitler, a man whose vision led millions into darkness and despair. How far it fell. People can easily forget the sacred when led astray by the profane.

And if this is true of nations, how much more of the individual?

Now, here I am. Standing at the edge of my own life's shoreline, looking back. I see the footprints I left behind scattered across the sands of memory. Some are deep and sure, others shallow and hesitant. But already, I can see the tide rising. The waves of time come rolling in, unrelenting, and those steps, those moments that once defined me, are being washed away. Erased as if they never were.

And I wonder... will anything remain?

Chapter 17
The Passing Time

April 23rd.

Today, the air is filled with the gentle strains of timeless music: fragments of symphonies, haunting piano nocturnes, and soaring arias that seem to rise from another world. I sit quietly, wrapped in the spell of melodies composed by the great masters. Beethoven, Chopin, Mozart, and so many others whose hands once touched ivory keys and parchment with a kind of divine fire. Each note feels like a whisper from the past, echoing through the corridors of time, soft and persistent.

There is a warmth in revisiting these familiar sounds. It feels like returning to an old home in memory. I let the music wash over me, again and again, with a kind of reverence, as though each listen allows me to touch the souls of those long gone. And yet, a deep ache settles in my chest, a sadness hard to name. The very creators of this beauty, the ones who once breathed and dreamed and felt deeply enough to translate it into something eternal, are now silent. Like so many others from ages past, their voices have fallen away into the hush of history, taken by the angel of death.

I find myself wondering. Where are they now?

Are they in some luminous realm, embraced by the divine presence they may have longed for? Or are they, like us, waiting quietly and curiously for judgment, for justice, for something more? I imagine the kings and poets, the prophets and painters, the nameless and the famous, gathered in a strange, otherworldly hush. Is there a conversation among them? Do they speak of what once was, of glory and failure, of laughter, of regrets? Do they remember their lives as we remember them, flawed, magnificent, fleeting?

These thoughts rise unbidden, looping in my mind like a broken reel of film. I know how fanciful it all sounds. Maybe I am simply spinning tales in a world only I inhabit, a private reverie where memory, music, and mystery entwine. Still, the questions come like waves. They do not seek resolution but ache to be asked.

And perhaps that is the point. To wonder is to feel, and to feel is to remember that we, too, are part of this strange and beautiful story.

Chapter 18
Melodies of the Heart

There is something undeniably human about the desire to express ourselves, a quiet, persistent longing that lives deep within our souls. It doesn't always seek a stage or an audience. Sometimes, it simply wants to be heard by one person, someone who truly listens. If we could, perhaps we'd each sing a song that belongs only to us, a private melody formed by the contours of our lives. A tune so unique that no one else would recognize it, yet so honest that anyone listening would feel it in their bones.

I often imagine what it would be like if we met someone; our feelings emerged not through awkward conversation or forced gestures but as music, a spontaneous song that told the truth of our hearts. A melody that said, *This is who I am. This is what you mean to me.* How powerful that would be. And yet, how vulnerable, too.

Of course, such a world would come with its own discomforts. There would be moments of embarrassment, even pain, when someone's melody revealed more than they wished or when we heard a song we were not ready for. But still, the beauty of it, the idea that no emotion need be buried, that nothing would be lost in translation, is deeply moving.

In our real, quieter world, we express ourselves through words, gestures, acts of kindness, and sometimes just the way we sit in silence beside someone. And though these expressions are imperfect, they are still profoundly meaningful. Yet I often carry the weight of missed moments; those times I held back, didn't speak, didn't show enough. Especially when someone is gone and the chance has passed forever. It leaves a hollow space that nothing quite fills, a silence where a song should have been.

Memory becomes a kind of echo then. A distant refrain of what might have been. And all we can do is try to be more present with those who remain. To reach out more freely. To say the things that need saying. To love in ways that leave no room for regret.

The word "love" has become a worn garment, pulled over too many moments that other names should have called. What passes for love is sometimes no more than fleeting infatuation, a rush of affection without depth. People meet, feel a spark, and before truly seeing one another, they rush into promises their hearts aren't yet ready to keep. And when the illusion fades, silence and sorrow are often left. The kind of loneliness that cuts deeper because it follows something that once felt so alive.

But still, I believe in love. I believe in the kind of love that grows slowly and speaks quietly. A love that isn't always declared loudly but is shown through gentle consistency, understanding, through forgiveness. A love that sings not the loudest song but the truest one.

I hope that there is a melody like that within each of us, a real melody of love. Not a performance but a presence. One that, when shared, can ease another's loneliness, lift a weary spirit, and make this complicated world just a little softer.

Because somewhere out there, someone may be waiting to hear our song. And we might be the only music they need.

Chapter 19
Look, Look inside

What do we really see when we look at him?

An old man sits alone. The lines etched into his face are not merely the result of age but the quiet remnants of a thousand silent battles. Perhaps his eyes, once bright, are now dulled by time and memory. They seem to look past the world rather than at it, not searching anymore, just drifting. To a passerby, he might seem like any other elder, slowly moving through the rhythms of survival. But if you look closely, you'll notice something else. He is not quite living. He is existing.

He wakes, eats, sleeps, breathes. And that is it. No laughter rises unprompted, no spark of curiosity that lights up his expression. Whatever joy once danced in his spirit has been quieted. Whatever fire once burned in his chest now flickers low, almost out of reach.

What happened to him?

The journey from youth to this quiet unraveling is not written in a single chapter. It is the slow erosion of hope. The steady weight of disappointment layered upon disappointment until the body is upright one day, but the soul is curled into itself. Maybe it was heartbreak, the kind that never heals. Maybe he trusted the wrong people or simply lived too long trying to meet the impossible expectations of others. Perhaps it started early, with parents who loved more through discipline than warmth, who carved strict lines into his path and left no space for dreams. Maybe he followed the rules so closely that he forgot how to feel.

Or perhaps the truth is more haunting. Perhaps the damage was already there, a quiet shadow within him from the beginning. Something inherited or inexplicably seeded deep in his bones. A sorrow he could not name, only carry.

The questions are endless. Each one circles the others, never quite touching the core. And maybe he, too, has spent sleepless nights asking himself, How did I get here? Was this always inside me, waiting to unfold?

There is a kind of tragedy in the realization that the person we become is not always the person we imagined in our youth. When we are young, we see life as a vast horizon, waiting. Then life happens. And for some, like him, it happened hard. It stripped him of softness. It dulled his wonder. It taught him to survive but not how to heal.

And yet, there is still something human about him. There is a quiet, aching dignity even in this hollowed version of who he might have been. A story left unsaid. Maybe even a last flicker of yearning.

He is not just a shell. He is what remains after a storm. And while he may never again be who he once hoped to be, maybe he still holds the silent possibility of grace within him. Maybe he is still asking the questions, and there is a sliver of life in the asking.

Because even in the emptiest rooms of the heart, sometimes, if we listen closely enough, we can still hear the echo of who we were and who we might have been.

Chapter 20
Where Has My Heart Wandered Off To?

It has gone into this unknown world.

The sights I see are alien and strange.

I try to touch that unreachable, but cannot.

What is it that beckons me to go further,

To go deeper and deeper into that great abyss,

Where all thoughts are stored and where memories,

From so long ago, are buried and forgotten?

I shiver to think what I may dig up there.

Where is the part where love is stored?

Oh, there it is. It is a large box, and when I

Opened it, it says, "Love of self," and it startles me.

Am I like that? No, really, it must be a mistake.

I loved a lot of people, and now this?

Get me out of here and let me think about this

For a while, as surely I know what love is.

Or have I had it wrong all these many years?

Turning inward, I experience a strange feeling

Of inadequacy, of having been left behind,

While others expressed their love so freely,

And I, holding back that essential part of life

That gives meaning to everything around me.

I see it now, and as I stand back and look at myself,

I am suddenly overpowered by a force that opens

The eyes of my blind heart, and now love rushes in,

And goes into every crevice of my being, and I

Become like what others have always been,

Alive again forevermore, with love to spare.

Chapter 21
The Wish

Needless to say, a wish alone does not make something come true. It is a soft whisper against the roar of reality. I often think of it like a person with no legs yearning to walk. The longing is real; the will is powerful, but the body simply cannot follow. There is a chasm between desire and ability that many of us live with quietly every single day.

Sometimes, I look around and see people whose abilities seem to stretch beyond my own, not only in talent or intellect but in moral strength as well. They carry themselves with a kind of light like they've made peace with the world in a way I never quite could. If I'm honest, some of them seem almost angelic in the way they navigate life – graceful, unburdened, steadfast. And I can't help but feel small by comparison.

But I will not despair. I remind myself that, in the end, we all arrive at the same stillness. The same place beyond time and form. We will all pass on no matter who we were and what we achieved or failed to achieve. And when we do, what remains – if anything – is the imprint of our existence. A whisper of our presence, carried forward not by monuments or fame but by the lives we've touched.

For me, that legacy lives in my children. They carry my blood, stories, imperfections, and quiet hopes. It moves through them like a silent current, as it once moved through my father and his father before him. There is something sacred in that continuity, even if it is unseen. Though we leave this world, we do not vanish. We ripple forward.

Sometimes, I worry I am rambling, that these thoughts might seem scattered to anyone reading them. But they come from a sincere place. And if even one person finds something familiar in these reflections, something that makes them pause and say, *"Yes, I've felt that too,"* then it's worth writing down. We often forget how alike we are in our silent moments and how many of us carry the same questions just beneath the surface.

Each of us is a singular creation. Even if there are others who look like us, sound like us, live in similar places, or walk similar paths, the soul within each of us is utterly unique. There will never be another person quite like you or me in the history of the world. That thought is humbling and oddly comforting in all its quiet wonder.

The other day, I found myself drifting into memories. I was thinking about the movie stars I used to admire in my younger years. Their faces were once everywhere – glowing on the silver screen, larger than life, immortal in their beauty and charm. And now I wonder... where are they? What became of those luminous lives? Are they still remembered? Are they still here at all?

The world moves on so fast. Time erases even the brightest lights if we're not careful. But in moments like this, when we pause and reflect and speak the names of those who meant something to us, something extraordinary happens. We bring them back for a moment. We allow them to live again, not in fame, but in memory. In gratitude.

And maybe that's all we ever really need – to be remembered with kindness and to know that, somehow, our presence mattered to someone.

In the quiet hours of thought, I often wonder whether there might be a special place in heaven where movie stars gather together. A timeless corner of eternity where they can sit side by side, remembering the glimmer of the spotlight, the thrill of applause, and the joy of creating moments that once touched millions. I imagine them conversing, laughing softly about old scenes, and sharing stories from long-dismantled sets. Perhaps they are reunited not as celebrities but as souls who once brought a little more beauty into the world.

Or perhaps it is not like that at all. Perhaps we will all find ourselves in a place of stillness, a space where time no longer matters, waiting quietly for the day of reckoning, when each of us will be seen for who we truly are. Not for our fame or our failures but for the choices we made, the love we gave, and the hearts we touched.

When I sit down to watch an old movie, as I often do, something tender stirs in me. The screen lights up, and suddenly, they are there again. The stars of the past. Their voices echo from another era. Their smiles are bright. Their movements are full of life. And for a moment, I forget that they are gone. But then the thought returns, gentle yet painful. They are no longer walking this earth. They are gone, and it breaks my heart.

Sometimes, I cannot help but weep. These people who once dazzled the world, who seemed so full of promise and spirit, now exist only in the flicker of film and the fading recollection of those who still remember them. They live again, briefly, as the reel turns and the music swells. And then the credits roll, and they fade once more.

I wonder what it would be like for someone who has never seen a movie, someone from a place untouched by film or television. If such a person were to sit and watch these moving images for the first time, they might believe the stars are alive, living out their stories in real-time. There would be no sense of loss, only the wonder of discovery. To them, these actors would not be memories. They would be present. Breathing. Real.

And that is the strange magic of memory. It keeps the past alive in ways nothing else can. A photograph, a melody, or a line from a film can transport us to a place that no longer exists, with people who are no longer here. We hold on to these fragments because they remind us of who we were and what we felt. They carry the weight of love, of nostalgia, of longing.

Yet time moves without mercy. Whether a thousand years have passed or only a second, what has gone is truly gone. The moment is over. The scene has ended. And nothing, no matter how powerful, can bring it back.

Still, in remembering, there is something sacred. We honor the past not by trying to relive it but by allowing it to shape us, soften us, to teach us how fleeting and precious every heartbeat truly is.

When I look toward the future, I am struck by the humbling realization that I know nothing about it. Not really. No matter how much I try to prepare, no matter how much I plan or worry, the next second remains hidden from me, untouched and unknowable. It slips quietly out of reach just as I begin to imagine it.

Time is a strange companion. It walks beside us, yet always ahead of us. It holds us in its grasp without mercy or pause. We are bound to it, tethered to its silent forward march. And though we may believe we can shape it, time does not bend to our will. Yes, we can make small choices. We can decide to stop smoking, to go on a diet, to welcome a child into the world. We can shift the rhythm of our days. But still, what is meant to unfold often finds its way to us, no matter the detours we try to take.

Sometimes, I think of those who came before us, the great rulers of history who stood atop empires and watched civilizations rise and fall. Alexander the Great, with all his ambition and vision. The emperors of Rome were surrounded by grandeur and fear. Genghis Khan crossed continents with fire and fury. They believed, perhaps, that they were changing the world. And they did, in their time. They moved borders. They shifted the course of nations. But now, they are gone, like dust swept into the corners of history. And I wonder, did it really matter in the end? Did all that striving and conquering leave behind anything more lasting than a few lines in the pages of a textbook?

Life continues. With or without glory. With or without freedom. People live in joy and in sorrow, in sickness and in health. Some are born into peace, others into pain. Some walk with ease, others stumble forward without limbs. And yet, life goes on. It does not wait. It does not pause for the weary or the wondering. It presses forward like a river that cannot be stopped.

I find myself thinking about this often. Where does it all lead? Is there a final chapter to this story, a closing sentence waiting somewhere ahead of me? Or will I simply fade into the current, like so many before me, becoming a part of the flow, forgotten by all but a few?

There are days when I sit in the quiet, lost in these thoughts. I watch the sunlight spill across the floor and listen to the faint ticking of the clock. Each sound reminds me that time is still moving, and I am still here. I do not know how many more pages I have left to write in the book of my life. But I am here now. I breathe. I wonder. I hope.

And perhaps, for this moment, that is enough.

Chapter 22
Nothingness

The fist of anger raised, will not be raised again

The angry words, once spoken, will be heard no more

The proud are now so lowly bound

When they are put into the ground

The singing lark will now fall silent

The ear that heard can hear no more

And blind the eye that saw so much

There will be an all compassing silence

As all who were, will be no more

No more, no more, no more, no more

Because we'll sleep forevermore.

Chapter 23
Homeward Bound

I am homeward bound, my love. Don't leave me on the way,

but stay with me until the end comes and my life is done.

The road I am on is not too hard, but full of curves going off

Into another direction where no exits are, and the end so dreary

That I don't want to wander off into a world that's alien to me.

I know with my broken wings, I can't go far, as I am a prisoner of my past.

From which there seems to be no escape, but I have to try.

And make it to where I am going just the same, so going on I must.

The sparrow still sings in yonder tree, so life goes on also for me.

The ants are still busy building and caring for their offspring

And the bee is still visiting the flowers to maintain their existence. The leaves are

still green, and don't know the fall is on the way that will change them all into a

brilliant color that will be seen by all with an eye for these changes and enjoys them.

As for me, what am I sulking about? I am still able to see and hear the birds and

should not be so morose, as there is still lots to do and the soul is still within me,

and departure may be still years away. When I look back on the road
I once traveled

and see all the ruins of my life, I come to the conclusion that even
though it is all

a memory, the strong vision seems to be so real that I am scared all
over again, and

my life comes to a standstill once more, and the overpowering
feelings come to the

fore and leave me so sad, but I must go on with a strong heart and
sober mind, and so

I will.

Chapter 24
My Youth

When I was young, and looked at the world through the eyes of a youngster and saw it like a big ball of candy and could not get enough of the great taste of it. When I was getting older, I realized that all was not sugar and spice, but that the world was more of a place where there was not always peace, and that the people you knew were not always what they seemed to be, but that they became more like grown-ups every day.

My dear parents tried to prepare me for the world to come and gave me advice on many things; however, I thought I knew it all and was prone not to listen to them as I should have. As a teenager, I was somewhat rebellious and would do things not on the up and up. I sometimes got in trouble with the law for my misbehavior, but I was lucky to have an understanding judge who let me off with a warning. As I got older and developed an eye for girls, I became more mellow, and sexual thoughts were never far from my mind, not realizing that this was only a byproduct of a true and lasting relationship. The temporary relations with some girls ended, and then the one came into my life. My love for her blossomed into a full-blown affection.

Chapter 25
Another poem

When I look up into the sky

And see the Milky Way

I often wonder why

And don't know what to say

I feel so little and so small

But never feel forlorn

Cause I am greater than it all

I live and I was born

The universe is dead to me

Though beauty shows at night

No star will ever like me to be

Alive when this I write.

Chapter 26
More Thoughts and Angst

To say to oneself, *"Woe is me,"* is not easy. It becomes even more difficult when we live with the knowledge that one day, we will stand before Almighty God and give an account of our lives. This truth weighs heavily on my heart. I am fully aware of it, yet I still struggle to embrace the reality of God's forgiveness for me. I continue to sin every day. With each passing day, the weight of my wrongdoing grows heavier, and my soul feels more burdened.

These sins are not limited to my personal failures. I have wronged my own family and those who placed their trust in me. The number of people I have hurt is overwhelming. I have run out of excuses and cannot shift the blame onto anyone else. I am the one at fault. The thought of so many voices rising in the hereafter to accuse me fills me with fear. I imagine them standing before God, testifying against me, and declaring the pain I caused them. According to justice, I deserve condemnation. I deserve hell because of the way I have lived… careless, thoughtless, and often selfish. My words and actions have hurt others deeply.

What makes my guilt even more painful is that I have always considered myself someone who understands religion. I have written books about God and spiritual life. I have spoken of faith and truth. Yet now, none of that can excuse what I have done. I will not be able to say, "I did not know." I knew. And still, I failed.

At times, I find myself speechless. Saying "I am sorry" feels inadequate. Even if I were to offer my life in repentance, it would not undo the harm I have caused. The damage is already done, especially to those closest to me. My sorrow feels too deep for words.

When I look at others, I feel they are all better than I am. Everyone around me seems more faithful, more kind, more disciplined, and more honest. I feel like I have wasted the gifts I was given. I feel like I have failed my calling. I feel like I have failed God.

Yet, despite all of this, I hold onto one final hope. That hope is found in Jesus Christ, the Savior of all who turn to Him with a sincere heart. Only He can undo what I have done. Only He can carry the burden of my sin and cleanse me from my guilt. He bore the sins of the world on the Cross. He alone can bear mine as well. He forgave the thief, the adulterer, and even those who crucified Him. Can He not also forgive me?

Still, I feel that God is distant. It is as though He has hidden His face from me. I am lonely, lost, and far from the peace I once knew in His Word. My heart longs for Him. In the quiet hours of the night, I cry out to Him. I ask Him to come near. I ask Him to open my blind eyes and soften my heart before it is too late. One day, I will lay down my head and not rise again. I do not want to leave this world still trapped in shame and regret.

The words of the Apostle Paul echo in my mind. "I do not understand what I do. For what I want to do, I do not do, but what I hate, I do." And again, "O wretched man that I am! Who will rescue me from this body of death?" These verses capture my struggle perfectly.

As we grow older, the dreams we once held… the visions of greatness and achievement… begin to slip away. The daily routines of life become what remains. The excitement and passion that once fueled our days begin to fade. This change happens so gradually that we often do not notice it. It is only when we pause, reflect, and look back that we become aware of what is slipping through our fingers.

In these moments of reflection, a sudden energy may awaken within us. Our eyes open again, and we gain a brief sense of clarity. We begin to see where we have come from and where we are going. For a little while, the path becomes clear. But soon, the distractions of life return, and that clarity fades again.

With time, our strength diminishes. Our bodies become fragile, and even the lightest burden can feel overwhelming. The smallest challenge can slow us down. I know that this experience is not shared by everyone. There are people who remain active, vibrant, and strong until the very end of their lives. I admire them deeply.

However, this is not my story. I am not like them, and I have come to accept that. This is who I am. In that realization, I find a strange kind of uniqueness. There is no one else exactly like me. My life, with all its joys and regrets, is singular. No one else has lived it or felt exactly what I have felt.

Perhaps that is what makes each human life so sacred. It is not about comparison or competition. It is about understanding that every person is a one-of-a-kind creation, never to be repeated. My experience is my own, and it matters, even in its weakness and imperfection.

I write these words not to seek pity or admiration but to speak honestly about what it means to grow older. There is sorrow in letting go of the dreams of youth, but there is also wisdom in recognizing the beauty of the present. I am still here. I am still breathing. That alone is a gift. Even if the fire burns more dimly than before, it still burns. And while there is life, there is still time to live meaningfully and to draw closer to the One who created me.

Chapter 27
The Slayer of Man

Let there be no doubt that the enemy of humanity is Satan and those who follow him. He was present from the beginning. He was a created being, just like the angels. His existence began when time, as we understand it, came into being. According to Scripture, Satan held a position of authority in heaven. He was responsible for music and had influence over many aspects of heaven.

Over time, pride entered his heart. He started to believe that he was equal to God. Eventually, he challenged God's authority and wanted to take God's place. This act of rebellion could not be allowed. God removed him from heaven, and one-third of the angels who sided with him were also cast out.

From that point forward, God's plan began to unfold. He created the universe and the earth. He formed a new creation: the human race. From this race, God would choose people with sincere hearts and a natural desire to seek and know their Creator. These individuals would live in fellowship with God and would take the place of the angels who had fallen.

This is not about humans replacing angels in the literal sense. Human beings were never angels and never will be. The point is that God created humanity with a purpose. But because of sin, people became separated from God. Reconnection with Him could not happen through effort or goodness alone.

This is why Jesus Christ, the Son of God, had to come into the world. He became the way through which people could be restored to God.

Without Him, no one can be saved. He is the only way to eternal life. Through His death and resurrection, He paid the price for sin and made it possible for people to be forgiven and made right with God.

His atoning work is what cleanses us, as believers in the Savior, from all our wrongdoing and every sin we have committed during our time on this earth. We had no way of saving ourselves. It is as though we were standing at a distance, completely unable to bridge the gap between us and God. Yet Christ stepped in and fulfilled everything that was required for our salvation.

We are not worthy, not even to loosen the strap of His sandal. There is nothing in us that could earn or deserve the grace that has been given. But through His death on the cross, Jesus made us worthy in the eyes of God. He took our place. He carried our guilt. He satisfied the justice of God so that we could be forgiven.

There was no other way for us to be reconciled to the Father. No amount of good works, knowledge, or religious effort could have opened the door to Heaven. Only the sacrifice of Christ—perfect, voluntary, and complete—could make that possible.

Through Him, we are given access to God. Through Him, we are no longer strangers or condemned sinners. We are made children of God, not by anything we have done but by what He has done for us.

Chapter 28
The Struggles

What is it that has brought our world into the state it is in today? Everywhere we look, there are struggles. In the field of manufacturing, companies compete fiercely to produce the best product, to outperform their competitors, and to dominate the market. Success is often measured by profit, innovation, and reputation, and the pressure to stay ahead is relentless.

In politics, the struggle is for power and control. Political parties constantly claim that they have the answers to our problems. Leaders make promises, often speaking of change and solutions, but time and again, people are left disillusioned. The desire to govern has, in many cases, become more about influence and authority than true service to the people.

In sports, the struggle is to be the best. Teams and athletes dedicate their lives to training and competing for trophies and recognition. For some, victory brings pride and purpose. For others, it becomes just another pressure in a world already full of demands.

Then there is the daily struggle for survival. In many parts of the world, people face extreme poverty, hunger, disease, and violence. Their goal is not fame, power, or success but simply to make it through another day. Families suffer under broken systems, and many have no safety net or support.

Governments across the globe also struggle to maintain control. Some attempt to enforce systems like communism, fascism, or socialism, often suppressing dissent and imposing strict control over their populations. These systems can create tension, fear, and unrest when personal freedom is sacrificed in the name of order or ideology.

In the Middle East and other regions, conflict is ongoing. Some governments are under attack from radical groups seeking to replace them with religious regimes. These groups often use religion to justify violence and oppression. One cannot ignore the fact that extremist movements claiming to act in the name of Islam have brought instability to entire regions. Innocent people are being killed, including Muslims who oppose these radical interpretations. In many cases, the violence is not between religions but within them, as extremist factions attempt to seize power and enforce strict, oppressive rules.

These killings and acts of terror continue without end. Civilians are caught in the crossfire, and fear has become a normal part of daily life in many areas. This level of violence and destruction cannot be seen as anything but evil. There is a force at work that is not merely political or social but deeply spiritual. It thrives on chaos, hatred, and division.

When we stop and think about the past, it's hard not to remember the many civil wars that have happened in different countries. In each case, thousands and even millions of people lost their lives, often for the sake of a leader who wanted more power. Whether it was a dictator, a tsar, a king, or a political leader, many of them believed they were the right people to take control, even if it meant people had to die for it.

It also makes me think about the companies and people who make weapons. Year after year, new weapons are designed to be more powerful and more deadly. The goal always seems to be to kill more people, faster and more effectively. These weapons don't just target soldiers. They also kill innocent people who are caught in the middle. Homes, schools, hospitals, and entire towns are often destroyed without warning.

We've already seen two world wars, and the number of people who were killed, wounded, or went missing is too high to count. The memorials in different countries show us how many lives were lost. But even after those massive wars, conflicts kept happening, and they still do today.

It makes me wonder when the world will finally say to the weapons industry and to every government involved, "This needs to stop." Yes, I know that a lot of people work in those factories, and taking that away could leave many without jobs. But isn't human life more important? If the weapons stopped being made, maybe the fighting would slow down or even stop. That may sound unrealistic, but if we don't think that way, then what hope do we have at all?

The sad reality is that people keep dying in wars not just because of politics but also because of hate. Some wars are started just because one group has a different religion, culture, or skin color. People are being wiped out for things they have no control over. It's not right, and it's painful to watch.

I know that world peace is probably not going to happen in our lifetime. People are too divided, and power, money, and fear keep getting in the way. But that doesn't mean we should give up trying. We need to speak up, to ask questions, and to stop pretending that war is normal.

Real peace won't come by itself. It will only happen if enough people truly want it and are willing to work for it, even if it's just in small ways. Until then, all we can do is keep trying to do what's right and not turn away from the truth, no matter how hard it is to face.

Chapter 29
Pearls of wisdom

A day without sunshine is a nice day, too

The hearing of laughter can be a curse to some

An inquiring mind is an opening flower

In a child, we see eternity

A dog's wagging tail shows pleasure

What good is a ship without a rudder

A small act may lead to big things

Easy to please is an excellent trait

A cause can convert millions

Rapture is outrageous laughter

Freedom is normal for those who don't see

To take and not return gives off a foul odor

A blowhard has no wind

A narrow mind has on blinkers

The straight and narrow road is full of curves

To belong is a great gift

Time will cover all wrongdoings

The universe is full of droplets depending on one's size

The weak may be stronger than they think

Rubber stretches only so far

A lark not heard still sings

A blessing can be a curse

A new dawn brings endless complications

Hope is an unseen thing

Good is the absence of evil

Even the strong have weak spots

All oceans consist of droplets

Mountains disappear one grain at the time

Some hours are long, and some are short

One second can be a lifetime

A giant can be small in one's eyes

Envy is Satan's helper

Growth is that which comes natural

Debris are building blocks

Beyond is out of reach

Chapter 30
The Dead Are Alive In Our Hearts

To the thirsty, one drop of water is worse than no drink

The good old days are now, but we just don't see this

An erupting volcano is the earth's anger

Fire cleanses all things

Realism is the harsh reality

A Christian foregoes all rights

A double mind is like a candle in the draft

Progress is a step away from inertness

A title does not make the man

The morning has a mouthful of gold

Chapter 31
The World

As I sit here quietly and think about life, I start to understand just how limited we really are. Our eyes can only see what is nearby, and our ears can only hear what is close. Yet somehow, we walk around feeling like we are important like we have control over things. The truth is, the world is moving through space at an incredible speed. Even the ground beneath us is spinning at over a thousand miles per hour. Still, we act like we are at the center of everything. We hold on to the idea that we are somebody when, in reality, we are tiny pieces of something far bigger than we can truly understand.

When I think about history, I feel overwhelmed. So many terrible things have been done in the name of power. People have caused pain for kings, governments, tribes, or even their own families. It is painful to realize how often people have believed that if they themselves were safe, then it did not matter what happened to others. That kind of thinking feels cold and selfish. It is upsetting to see how easily people ignore the suffering of others just because it is not happening to them.

Looking back at the past, it becomes clear that even the greatest empires that once ruled huge parts of the world are now gone. Some ruins are still standing, but the power those empires held is long finished. What is really heartbreaking is the cost. So many young people were sent to fight and die for these empires, thinking they were protecting something important. But over time, those sacrifices often seem pointless. The rulers are gone. The borders have changed. And the lives that were lost can never be recovered.

Even today, the world is still caught in the same painful patterns. Some groups try to force others to follow strict religious or political rules. They believe that everyone must obey or be punished. That way of thinking is frightening. It feels like we have not learned anything from all the pain in our history. People still try to control others through fear and violence instead of kindness and understanding.

When I hear about acts of violence like bombings and attacks that kill not only outsiders but also people from the same religion or community, it leaves me feeling deeply sad and confused. It is hard to understand how anyone can believe that such actions are right. It feels like there is no care left for human life. In places where strict systems take control, ordinary people often suffer the most. They live in fear, they lose loved ones, and they grow up surrounded by pain and confusion.

I am not saying these things to attack any religion or culture as a whole. I understand that most people, no matter where they come from or what they believe, want to live in peace, raise their families, and be treated with basic respect. But there are still groups that use fear and violence to control others, and that needs to be recognized and challenged. We have to speak honestly about the harm being done, not just in the past but right now in the present.

What troubles me deeply is how fast the past is forgotten. The mistakes, the suffering, and the lessons are ignored. People focus only on what they want today and forget what came before. That kind of thinking puts everyone in danger. It keeps the cycle of pain going and leaves people feeling powerless, like their voices and their lives do not matter.

I have come to understand that many of the violent acts we see today, especially those committed by extremists who claim to follow Islam, often seem aimed at weakening or destabilizing governments that do not fully follow the teachings of the Koran. These attacks do not happen randomly. They are part of a larger effort to spread a certain way of life, one that is deeply tied to strict religious beliefs. It is deeply troubling to watch this unfold, especially when the leaders of some Islamic groups openly say that they intend to see Western countries become Islamic states in the future.

This may sound like an exaggeration to some, but the numbers support the concern. In certain cities in Europe, some schools now have more than half of their student population made up of children from Muslim families. One of the major reasons for this rapid population growth is tied to family structure. In some Islamic traditions, a man is allowed to marry more than one wife, sometimes two, three, or even four. This naturally leads to more children being born in those families, compared to Western families, where most people marry only one spouse. You do not need to be a mathematician to understand the long-term impact this can have on the culture, values, and identity of a nation.

It leaves me wondering if there is any real solution. Can a Western country change its laws to stop people from having multiple wives? And if so, would such laws even be respected or followed? Could immigration policies be changed to limit or stop people of the Islamic faith from entering, and would that even be fair or legal? These are very difficult and emotional questions. They touch on human rights, freedom of religion, and the right of people to build a better life for themselves and their families. It is not a matter of simple answers. It is a matter filled with fear, confusion, and the struggle to balance freedom with safety.

I am also haunted by what I saw as a boy. I remember the Jewish people being taken from their homes. They were forced into trucks, sent to concentration camps, and many were later killed in the Holocaust. I remember the fear and sadness that hung in the air, even for those of us who were not taken. That memory has stayed with me for my entire life. I hope and pray that we never repeat such cruelty. No one should be taken from their homes or sent away simply because of their faith or background. I fear, however, that if violence from extremist groups continues and more innocent people are hurt or killed, the anger of the Western world could grow in a dangerous direction. People might begin to blame all Muslims for the actions of a few, just as Jews were once blamed for the problems of others. That kind of thinking leads to dark places, and we must be careful not to go there again.

The attacks on September 11th were shocking and heartbreaking. Many people believed that day marked the beginning of a new kind of suffering. Since then, the world has become more divided, more suspicious, and more angry. Trust between people and nations is getting weaker. Many feel afraid and uncertain about the future. It is hard to feel safe when we see bombings, shootings, and other violent acts on the news almost every week. It is as if we are all sitting on a ticking clock, not knowing when or where the next explosion will happen.

Looking at history, it is clear that terrible things have been done by powerful nations again and again. For over two thousand years, wars have caused endless suffering. But today, because of how many people live on this planet and how advanced our weapons have become, the damage would be far worse than anything we have seen before. It takes only one decision, one missile, one bomb, and millions of lives could be lost.

I think about the end of World War II when the atomic bomb was dropped on Hiroshima and Nagasaki. In just a few seconds, tens of thousands of people were killed. Many more died in the weeks that followed from burns, sickness, and radiation. That event changed the world forever. Now, we have weapons that are many times more powerful than those first bombs. If such weapons are used in a future war, we would not be talking about tens of thousands of deaths. We would be talking about millions, maybe even entire nations, being wiped out in a matter of minutes.

I feel strongly that we are standing on the edge of something very dangerous. A war of such size and force that it could be unlike anything humanity has ever faced. I believe that the state of Israel will be caught in the middle of this conflict. There are tensions between Israel and groups from the Islamic world, and also growing conflict involving countries like Russia and China. If these powerful forces collide, the outcome could be beyond what most people can imagine.

In my mind, it is almost certain that nuclear weapons will be used if this kind of war happens. This would mark not just the end of a war but possibly the end of an era. It could destroy the world as we know it. Maybe, from the ashes of such destruction, something new would rise. Some people speak of a new age coming, perhaps something like the Age of Aquarius, a time of renewal and change. But before any of that, there will be great loss, pain, and struggle.

I do not say these things to spread fear. I say them because I care. I care about the world we live in. I care about the people who live here. I hope that we can still learn, change, and choose peace over destruction. But I also know that time may be short, and we must open our eyes before it is too late.

Chapter 32
An Inward Journey

Going on an inward journey is not easy, as it feels like admitting the truth about yourself. When I look back on my life and see all the broken promises and the wrong turns I have taken, I realize that many people behave much better than I do. It often seems like the whole world does.

Am I a coward? In many ways, I am. I avoid responsibility and would rather let others do the hard work that helps make the world a better place. People have called me names that are not kind. I have often brushed these off as just angry reactions to things I may have done to them, maybe without even knowing it.

I may seem like a religious person, but am I really? Or is it just an act to make people believe I am something I am not? It feels like hiding in the dark and only stepping into the light when I have to, and even then, not showing my real self.

Sometimes, my thoughts are so bad that I pray for them to go away. But they don't. I cannot stop them. I know the German saying, "Die Gedanken sind frei," which means "thoughts are free." No matter how strong my will is, I cannot stop them from coming. These thoughts can be abusive and sometimes sexual. When I try to fight them, they seem to get stronger, and my willpower fails.

I often wonder if I am the only one who goes through this. Do other people have these same kinds of thoughts? Maybe even the old lady down the street or the young men next door?

And so, I come back to where I started... from the outside world to my inner self, which is often filled with confusion and unrest.

I was listening to the songs "My Country" and "Jerusalem," and I felt great respect for the people who gave their lives in war for their king and country. Then I ask myself: would I give my life for my country, or would I run and hide when the moment came?

I realize that we will all die one day. When that day comes, and we are clearly faced with that fact, will we be strong enough to face death with courage, as if we could stand against it with a sword in our hand, ready to fight the one who always shows up when someone dies?

Will I feel a deep curiosity to see what is on the other side... the place that so many songs talk about, that so many sermons describe, and that so many books try to explain? Some of these books and messages are gentle and comforting, while others are harsh and speak of hell and the pain that will come to those who are not saved.

It is easy to talk about this, but many people, especially in academic circles, find it hard to believe in anything beyond what they can see, touch, or understand. If they cannot prove it, they reject it and call it a story or a myth.

I have come to see that many people die without believing in anything. They go to their graves as agnostics, never knowing the way to salvation. I know this moves into the topic of religion, and maybe that is good, because I believe that is the main reason we are here on earth. Many others feel the same way.

The way to find salvation may not be the same for every religion. But there is always a way to express what we believe, just like I am doing now. The path to God is not easy. It takes effort and preparation before we can be in the presence of God. A person must be cleaned of the wrong things they have done in life. This is shown, at least in a symbolic way, by the practice in the Baptist faith, where the whole body is lowered into water to show that a person is being washed clean.

I will stop here for now and hope to return to this later.

Chapter 33
More Thoughts

I just finished watching the last night of the "Proms" in 2009 and was amazed by the love the British people showed for their country and queen. It always surprises me how all of this comes together. I have come to realize that from birth, a child born in a particular country is taught about their nation... what it represents and what it stands for.

In schools, children learn the history of their country, its achievements, and its past glories, if any. They sing patriotic songs to honor their nation and are taught what it takes to maintain its current state. They are taught about freedom and what is required to protect it.

In most countries, an army is maintained to stop the nation from being overrun by a neighboring country or another power that wants to enslave them. Sometimes, the sacrifices made by soldiers are extreme, as they lay down their lives to protect their country's freedom. From an early age, children... and later, adults... learn that sacrifices may be necessary.

The consequences of the First and Second World Wars were severe. Could they have been prevented, or would negotiations have made no difference to the Kaiser or to Hitler? I'm sure many debates have been held by those who know more than I do. Still, the outcomes seem as impossible to reverse as trying to put a broken egg back together.

Anywhere in the world, when a head of state becomes obsessed with achieving something no one else has done, history often repeats itself. We can look back to Genghis Khan, Attila the Hun, Napoleon, or any other ruler who tried to expand their empire for personal glory. These leaders likely would not have listened to reason. There were always people around them who supported their plans and wanted to be part of their success.

When you think about it, it seems that pride and greed are very fragile things that can grow into dangerous forces. Once these take over, love fades, and cruelty takes its place. Mercy disappears from the minds of those who follow orders from their generals. The cruelty carried out by conquerors, even in today's world, is still common.

Many of these acts are committed in the name of religion or out of pure hatred for others, simply because they follow a different faith or belong to a different race.

Chapter 34
Personal Business

We will now enter the inner life of a soul that has been around for nearly eighty years... from early childhood until now. How did I arrive at this point in my life after all the broken ruins of the past?

The memories of long ago are still quite active in my mind, though they feel far away. Over time, they seem to come back and sometimes even grow stronger, as new events become linked to those past experiences. Time can be a great deceiver, and the accuracy of memories can fade as the past drifts further into the distance.

Still, the reality we once lived was strong enough that what we felt and thought back then remains deeply rooted in our minds. We often wish we had a clear path back to the past, one where we could undo some of the choices we made... especially our mistakes. But, as we all know, that is not possible.

I understand that most of us struggle with certain things we do and wish we could erase them from our memory. But here we are, and the emotional baggage we carry stays with us. As I mentioned, the passage of time seems to ease the weight of those memories, and the past begins to fade. Yet now and then, something happens that brings it all back, and we feel like we are starting over again. And so the cycle continues.

Chapter 35
More and more thoughts

While listening to Bach's *Jesu, Joy of Man's Desiring* and other masterpieces, I felt alone... almost helpless... as I could only listen and enjoy the music. I try to imagine what the composer was thinking when he wrote these works, and I admire the talent it takes to create something so timeless.

As for myself... who am I, and what have I accomplished in this world? Yes, I have written a number of books and made a small mark in the world of authors, but compared to so many others, it feels like just a drop in the bucket.

The great composers of the past are no longer with us, yet their music lives on through those who can read and perform it. I often wonder where they are now. Are they in a place unknown to us until we, too, arrive there after death?

The spirit world feels distant, but we all know how quickly that can change. Many people woke up this morning not knowing it would be their last day... whether due to a car accident, a heart attack, or some other unexpected event. It's not a cheerful thought, I know, but it crosses my mind often, as if on its own.

I've been writing these short reflections on my computer, hoping they might help me understand myself better when I read them later. Sometimes, it feels as if I am standing at a distance, watching myself in a mirror. My good side doesn't look too bad, but the bad side is in a sorry state... and we won't dwell on that, for everyone's sake.

Chapter 36
My Song

My song is not beautiful but from the heart.

I really don't know where to start.

My heart speaks to me with its needs.

For love and happiness in deeds,

Who is the one who understands

The longing for the reaching hands?

The need for sunshine in my life,

From friends, my family, or wife.

Is there no ending to my sorrow?

Will there be no more for me tomorrow?

Why must I remain in want?

Why does no one understand?

Am I indeed an island now,

As I sit here with furrowed brow?

I realize that it is mostly me

Who stands aside and lets them be.

Chapter 37
Other thoughts

Whom have I here on this earth? Are there any who truly know me? God knows my heart, and I long to be within the gates of the heavenly Jerusalem, where I will be safe, and nothing can touch or frighten me. The burdens of sin and my earthly baggage will all be gone, and only my voice will be heard, singing praises to Him who died in my stead.

I can bring nothing with me, and anything I have done for the good of mankind or my fellow human beings is nothing compared to the sacrifice made by Him who laid down His life so that we may live forever. The greatness of this will only be fully seen and known when we are there in that safe haven.

The sight of God's Anointed will be too glorious for us to comprehend and will leave us speechless at first. Then, together with all the other souls, we will lift our voices in unison and praise His name, Emmanuel, forever.

I feel my life slipping away from me, and I sense that my time is close at hand. Why I feel this way, I cannot tell you, but it is as if I have a second sight. May the Lord have mercy on me, a terrible sinner who does not even deserve to unloose the latchet of His shoe.

Chapter 38
Serenity

As I walk on the beach of my hometown at the water's edge, I look back and see my footprints in the sand. It's like looking into the past as I see my trail fading in the distance. The thoughts I had then have already been forgotten. I follow my trail to where I am now as if moving from the past back into the present.

I can hear the waves softly lapping against the shore, and the seagulls are flying high above, soaring on the gentle breeze. Their cries may be directed at me for stepping into their world or perhaps just at each other. I don't know.

In the distance, I can see a ship slowly passing across the horizon. It seems to be standing still, but of course, it isn't. My shoes crunch the seashells scattered across the beach, but my eyes are not on them. I do not care, for my attention is fixed on the surroundings in this early morning hour.

There is no one around, and the serenity revives my soul. All unpleasantness falls away as my eyes take in the vast expanse of sky and horizon. I try to become one with it all, to float away upon the gentle breeze and be carried to places as yet unseen. Try as I may, I am earthbound, and I pity myself for not being able to do this.

As I approach the ramp where people enter the beach, I see some coming now. For a while, I thought this beach was mine and that these people were intruding upon it. I hate to share this moment, but they have just as much right to be here as I do.

I turn around and begin retracing my steps, and with that, I disappear into the past to return once again to the present.

Chapter 39
Who and What is God

Why these questions arise in me, I don't really know. It seems that most people have the answers, except me. I was thinking about who and what God is and what He is all about. I do know one thing: the Godhead is not just one, but three in one, called the Elohim. There is no separation between them at any time.

These three existed from the beginning of time and, in fact, created time itself so that everything we see could come into being. This includes everything from the smallest atom to the greatest star or heavenly body in the universe. Seeing and understanding all of this should fill us with awe, especially when we reflect on ourselves and our so-called abilities.

God is not an old man with a beard. The Son and the Holy Spirit are not either. They exist in the fullness of strength, comparable to a person around the age of thirty, in our terms.

When God said, "Let us make man in our image," the word "us" referred to the Elohim. Humanity was created in strength, not as infants. As for Adam, I highly doubt he had a full-grown beard when he was created. Being male, he likely grew one later since razors had not yet been invented.

We often see images, paintings, or depictions of wise old men, including Jesus, with beards and beautiful features. However, many overlook Isaiah 53, where Jesus is described as being in poor health and of an appearance that we would not have desired.

Everything we see was created by the Son at the command of the Father. It is sustained by the Holy Spirit, who instilled in all things the laws that govern them. We often call these the laws of nature. They include what holds the atom together, magnetism, gravity, and all other forces that maintain the universe. Anything that has life is also governed by the laws placed within it from the beginning.

We do not have to look far to see this, from the smallest of plants to the greatest of animals. These laws govern everything, including us, and the functions of our bodies testify to this truth. The only part of us that is separate is our spirit or soul, if you prefer. It is subject to other forces that cannot be fully explained. However, we can say that evil forces are capable of influencing us to such a degree that we become slaves to whatever those forces intend for us.

It is at this point that belief in an Almighty being becomes essential. It is the only thing that prevents us from truly becoming slaves to evil. We must understand our eternal nature. This is the part of us that gives rise to the desire to become one again with the Elohim, where we once were when the worlds were formed. Our soul existed there, and within us is a longing to return to that unity with the Elohim.

The journey after birth on this earth is like a battleground. This is the result of the free will given to us following the fall of Adam and Eve. We carry many desires that aim to satisfy our earthly body. In doing so, we often forget the needs of our spiritual self, which longs for immortality and to return to the place we came from before we were born.

Let us observe nature and see how everything is regulated by forces that remain unknown to us. This is evident in the life of plants, animals, the planets, the stars, and the countless universes that have yet to be discovered. We see that everything has an end. Nothing lasts forever except the Elohim.

I will expand on the need for religious belief, as given to us by our Creator, and its purpose in our lives at another time.

Chapter 40
The Reason and Need for Religion

The question of why we need religion has been on many people's minds. From this, all the controversies surrounding the reasons for and against religion arise. Everyone has an opinion, and mine is this: if there is a God, there must be a way to contact Him. When we embrace a religion, perhaps we have found a way of doing just that.

To understand where religion comes from, we must go back as far as creation itself. Few people have not heard the story of Adam and Eve and their relationship with their Maker, God. This was the beginning of all the religions that exist today. They all have one thing in common: a God or Deity as their supreme being. Some call Him Allah, some refer to Buddha, and others use different names. With each of these come practices of worship through various rites and ceremonies.

The Christian faith also shares this origin. It begins with Adam, then his son Abel… who likely had offspring before he was slain by Cain… and continues through Enoch, Noah, Abraham, and the Israelites. From there, the tradition moved through Rome, the Reformation, and eventually to the King James Version of the Bible. In my opinion, this version provides the best translation from Greek, Hebrew, and other original languages.

I have come to believe that religion is a deeply personal matter. It involves faith in things unseen and is entirely a spiritual experience. We must come to terms with the fact that everything has an end, including our own lives. Then comes the question: what happens next? We must recognize that the promise of eternal life is not an empty one. Attaining it is crucial if we hope to receive it.

The Bible is a teaching tool given to us by God. He calls on us to read it in order to gain insight into His workings through the Holy Spirit and through Christ, who is the door by which we may enter the realm where all things are made clear. In this place, we are offered the assurance of eternal life, freely and without conditions.

I have observed that certain words carry more power than others, as is the case in all subjects. It is a gift to be able to read and understand the deeper meaning of written words. Some people possess the ability to express ideas eloquently, and we must admire that talent. I, too, in my own humble way, attempt to share with the reader why religion came into the world.

Chapter 41
Who, What and Were

Who am I, and what is my purpose in this life? Is it simply to be born, go through childhood, become a teenager, and then grow into adulthood? Now that I am an adult, what exactly am I, and what have I become? Have all the experiences I have had up to this point shaped me into a responsible person?

Life seems to move in a direction we cannot control. It continues, and whatever comes our way must be accepted as it is. A young man or woman may enter our life, and suddenly everything changes. Hormones begin to stir, and we believe ourselves to be in love or deeply attracted to that person. Before we know it, we are married, and children are on the way.

I know I am moving quickly through these stages, but I am trying to reach the point I truly want to make. It concerns our eternal soul, which is, whether we acknowledge it or not, an inseparable part of who we are.

So, what about this soul or entity, if you prefer? Countless books have been written on this subject, and religions since the beginning of time have explored this part of our being. Whether you are a Muslim, a Hindu, a Christian, or follow another faith, you will find an abundance of writings on this topic.

It is a reality that some people in this world are what we call "bad," while others are considered "good." I have often wondered whether there are also people who are "neutral"... neither good nor bad... who simply exist among us, going through life without taking a strong stance in any direction, holding no firm opinions, and passively accepting whatever happens around them.

When I look inward, I have to admit that I may be one of them. I tend to take things as they come. In a way, I feel disconnected from the world, even though there is still a flicker of interest in its events and in the news I watch on television. I often search for something meaningful in the headlines, but most of what I see involves violence and chaos.

There are too many people who seem to believe they will never die. They live only for the moment, doing whatever they want without concern for anything beyond the present. To them, life is about the here and now, and they give little or no thought to what lies beyond or to the concept of eternal life.

The atrocities committed by those in power are of an unspeakable nature, and to think that I, too, am part of this humanity, which is so often inhumane, is deeply troubling. What I am trying to say is that the difference between them and the rest of us is minimal, although it may not appear that way. When I reflect on all of this, I feel sorrow for the individuals who commit these acts, as they seem to have lost all feeling for the failings of others. Words like "love" and "compassion" likely never enter their minds.

I find myself thinking about people employed by a state or country who must fulfil roles in society... such as those responsible for executions in the past. Whether it was beheadings, hangings, or operating the electric chair, I wonder what they felt in those moments. I do not know. I am simply thinking out loud.

There seems to be no end to the violence. In today's world, suicide bombers are a new method of destroying innocent lives. The reasons may include religion, power, disruption, or possibly even the thrill of it... if such a term can be applied to murder. Some are driven by the promise of an afterlife that defies earthly understanding.

We stand as spectators, witnessing these horrors, and often, there is nothing we can do except report what we see and share what we experience. Anyone who believes in the existence of good and evil within mankind will likely conclude that this cannot continue indefinitely. A great cleansing, or reckoning, must occur. How it will happen, few can say, though many believe it will come through divine intervention.

At present, the internet is filled with voices claiming to have the answers. Many issue warnings of a global catastrophe they believe will take place in the near future. Whether or not to engage with these warnings is a personal choice. That is the question for those who read this book, and I hope they understand what I have tried to convey through my writing.

I lived through the Second World War as a child and witnessed many things no child should ever have to see. These experiences changed the way I think. At the same time, they taught me lessons that would prove valuable in my adult life.

www.ingramcontent.com/pod-product-compliance
Lightning Source LLC
Chambersburg PA
CBHW051218120626
46547CB00013B/1405